Excel for Beginners

EXCEL ESSENTIALS BOOK 1

M.L. HUMPHREY

ISBN: 978-1-950902-00-2

Also available under ISBNs 978-1538094662 and 978-1976480713

SELECT TITLES BY M.L. HUMPHREY

EXCEL ESSENTIALS
Excel for Beginners
Intermediate Excel
50 Useful Excel Functions
50 More Excel Functions

ACCESS ESSENTIALS
Access for Beginners
Intermediate Access

WORD ESSENTIALS
Word for Beginners
Intermediate Word

POWERPOINT ESSENTIALS
PowerPoint for Beginners
Intermediate PowerPoint

BUDGETING FOR BEGINNERS
Budgeting for Beginners
Excel for Budgeting

CONTENTS

INTRODUCTION

The purpose of this guide is to introduce you to the basics of using Microsoft Excel. I still remember when I was in college and helping a graduate student do research and he asked me to do something in Excel and I had no idea what to do and how frustrating that was to be limited by my lack of knowledge. I was later fortunate enough to work with a man who was absolutely brilliant with Excel who taught me lots of tips and tricks for using it and now I don't know what I'd do without it.

Excel is great. I use it both in my professional life and my personal life. It allows me to organize and track key information in a quick and easy manner and to automate a lot of the calculations I need. I have a budget worksheet that I look at at least every few days to track whether my bills have been paid and how much I need to keep in my bank account and just where I am overall financially. In my professional career I've used it in a number of ways, from analyzing a series of financial transactions to see if a customer was overcharged to performing a comparison of regulatory requirements across multiple jurisdictions. While it works best for numerical purposes, it is often a good choice for text-based analysis as well, especially if you want to be able to sort your results or filter out and isolate certain results.

If you want to learn Excel through the lens of managing your own money, the *Juggling Your Finances: Basic Excel Primer*, is probably a better choice. It walks you through how to do addition, subtraction, multiplication, and division using key questions you should be able to answer about your personal finances as the examples.

This book just focuses on the basics of using Excel without those kinds of specific examples. We'll cover how to navigate Excel, input data, format it, manipulate it through basic math formulas, filter it, sort it, and print your results.

This is not a comprehensive Excel guide. We are not going to cover more complex topics like conditional formatting and pivot tables. The goal of this guide is to give you a solid grounding in Excel that will let you get started using it. For day-to-day uses, this guide should cover 98% of what you need and I'll give you some tips on how to find the other 2 percent. (Or you can continue on with *Intermediate Excel* which covers more advanced topics like pivot tables, charts, conditional formatting, and IF functions.)

One note before we start: I'm working in Excel 2013, which will look familiar to users of Excel 2007 or later. If you're working in a version of Excel that's pre-2007, I'd recommend that you upgrade now rather than try to learn Excel in an older version. They're different enough that it's really like a completely different program.

If you do insist on using an older version of Excel, when I give you more than one method you can use (sometimes there are at least three ways to do the same thing in Excel), choose the option that tells you to right-click and open a dialogue box. Also, the Ctrl + [letter] options should be available in all versions of Excel. If that fails, use the help function to search for how the task can be completed in your version.

Alright then. Let's get started.

BASIC TERMINOLOGY

First things first, we need to establish some basic terminology so that you know what I'm talking about when I refer to a cell or a row or a column, etc.

Column

Excel uses columns and rows to display information. Columns run across the top of the worksheet and, unless you've done something funky with your settings, are identified using letters of the alphabet. As you can see below, they start with A on the far left side and march right on through the alphabet (A, B, C, D, E, etc.). If you scroll far enough to the right, you'll see that they continue on to a double alphabet (AA, AB, AC, etc.).

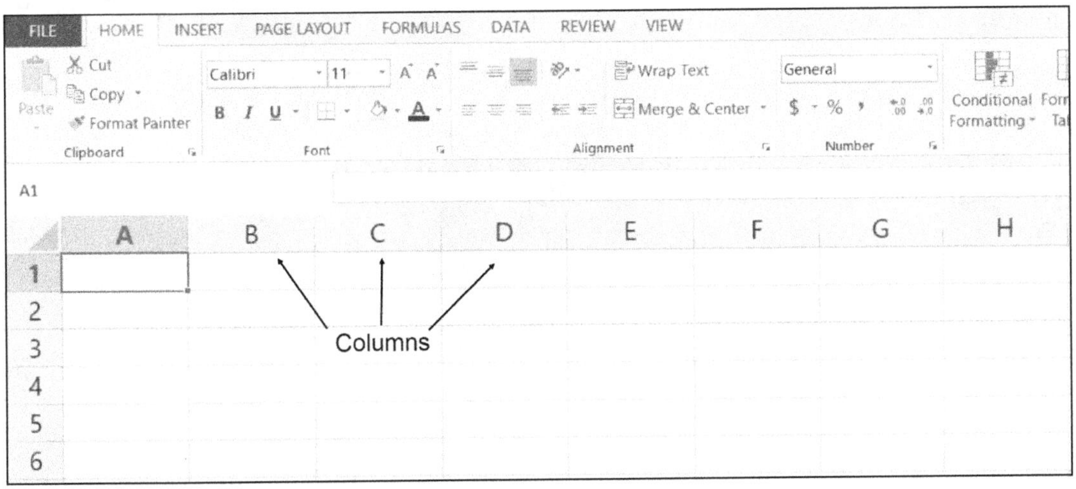

Row

Rows run down the side of the worksheet and are numbered starting at 1 and up to a very high number. You can hold down the ctrl key in a blank worksheet while hitting the down arrow to see just how many rows your version of Excel has. Mine has 65,536 rows per worksheet.

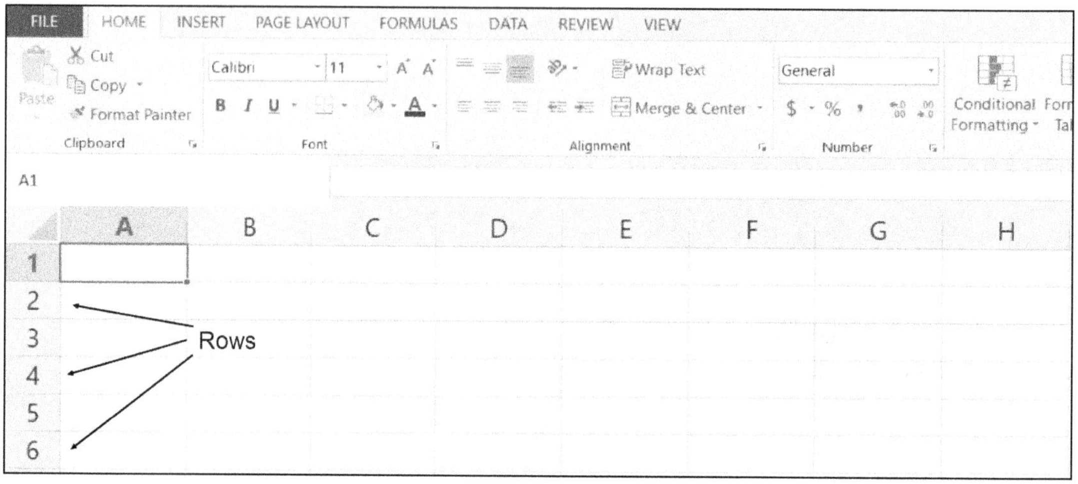

Cell

A cell is a combination of a column and row that is identified by the letter of the column it's in and the number of the row it's in. For example, Cell A1 is the cell in the first column and the first row of the worksheet. When you've clicked on a specific cell it will have a darker border around the edges like in the image below.

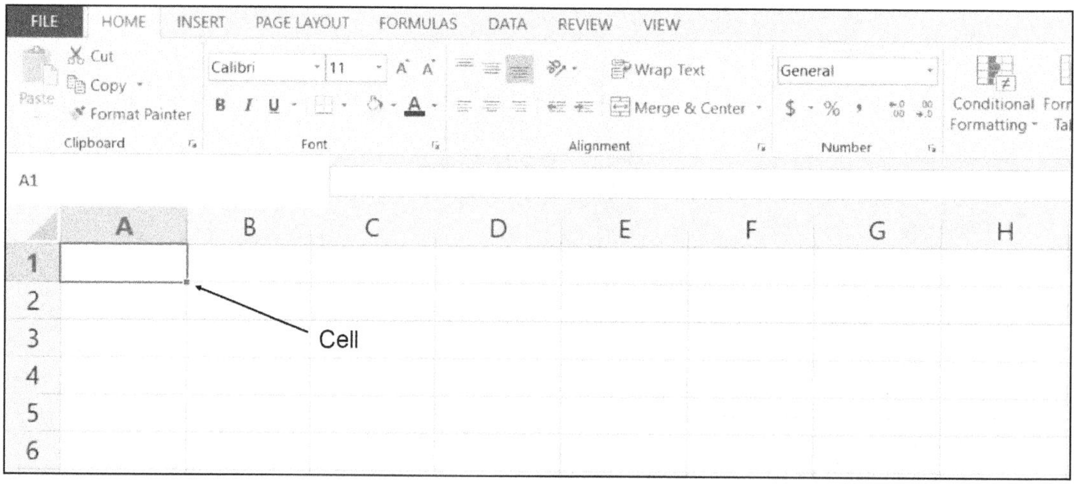

Click

If I tell you to click on something, that means to use your mouse (or trackpad) to move the arrow on the screen over to a specific location and left-click or right-click on the option. (See the next definition for the difference between left-click and right-click).

If you left-click, this selects the item. If you right-click, this generally creates a dropdown list of options to choose from. If I don't tell you which to do, left- or right-click, then left-click.

Left-click/Right-click

If you look at your mouse or your trackpad, you generally have two flat buttons to press. One is on the left side, one is on the right. If I say left-click that means to press down on the button on the left. If I say right-click that means press down on the button on the right. (If you're used to using Word or Excel you may already do this without even thinking about it. So, if that's the case then think of left-click as what you usually use to select text and right-click as what you use to see a menu of choices.)

Now, as I sadly learned when I had to upgrade computers and ended up with an HP Envy, not all track pads have the left- and right-hand buttons. In that case, you'll basically want to press on either the bottom left-hand side of the track pad or the bottom right-hand side of the trackpad. Since you're working blind it may take a little trial and error to get the option you want working. (Or is that just me?)

Spreadsheet

I'll try to avoid using this term, but if I do use it, I'll mean your entire Excel file. It's a little confusing because it can sometimes also be used to mean a specific worksheet, which is why I'll try to avoid it as much as possible.

Worksheet

A worksheet is basically a combination of rows and columns that you can enter data in. When you open an Excel file, it opens to worksheet one.

My version of Excel has one worksheet available by default when I open a new Excel file. (It's possible to add more as needed.) That worksheet is labeled Sheet 1 and the name is highlighted in white to show that it's in use.

Formula Bar

This is the long white bar at the top of the screen with the $f\chi$ symbol next to it. If you click in a cell and start typing, you'll see that what you type appears not only in that cell, but in the formula bar. When you input a formula into a cell and then hit enter, the value returned by the formula will be what displays in the cell, but the formula will appear in the formula bar when you have that cell highlighted.

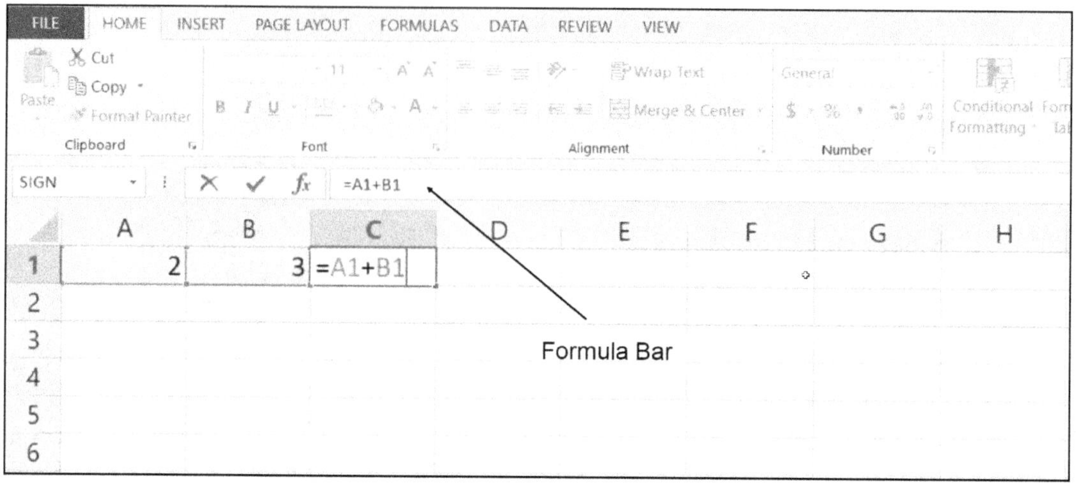

Tab

I refer to the menu choices at the top of the screen (File, Home, Insert, Page Layout, Formulas, Data, Review and View) as tabs. Note how they look like folder tabs from an old-time filing system when selected? That's why.

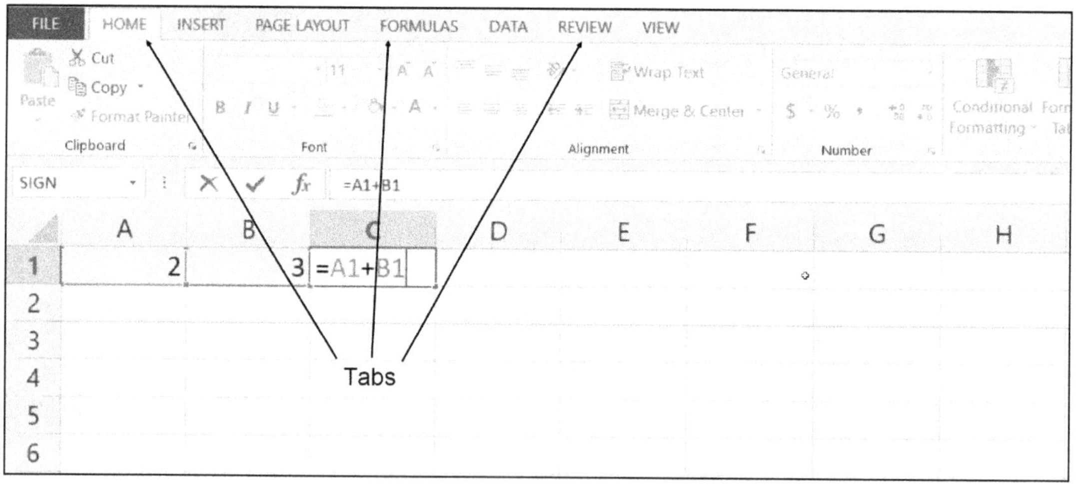

Each menu tab you select will show you different options. On my Home tab I can do things like copy/cut/paste, format cells, edit cells, and insert/delete cells, for example. (This is one place where things are very different for those using earlier versions of Excel and why if you're using an older version of Excel, I'd recommend upgrading now.)

Scroll Bar

On the right side and the bottom of the screen are two bars with arrows at the ends. If you left-click and hold on either bar you can move it back and forth between those arrows (or up and down for the one on the right side). This lets you see information that's off the page in your current view but part of the worksheet you're viewing.

You can also use the arrows at the ends of the scroll bar to do the same thing. Left-click on the arrow once to move it one line or column or left-click and hold to get it to move as far as it can go. If you want to cover more rows/columns at a time you can click into the blank space on either side of the scroll bar to move an entire screen at a time, assuming you have enough data entered for that.

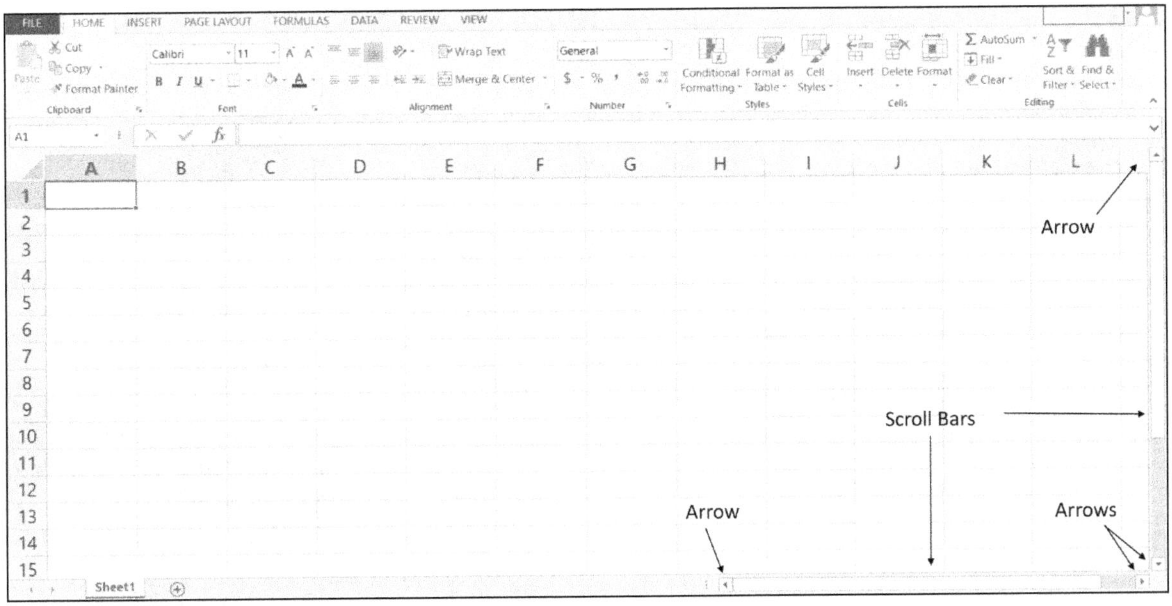

Using the arrows instead of clicking on the scroll bar lets you scroll all the way to the far end of the worksheet. Using the scroll bars only lets you move to the end of the information you've already entered.

Data

I use data and information interchangeably. Whatever information you put into a worksheet is your data.

Table

I may also refer to a table of data or data table on occasion. This is just a combination of rows and columns that contain information.

Select

If I tell you to "select" cells, that means to highlight them. If the cells are next to each other, you can just left-click on the first one and drag the cursor (move your mouse or finger on the trackpad) until all of the cells are highlighted. When this happens, they'll all be surrounded by a dark box like below.

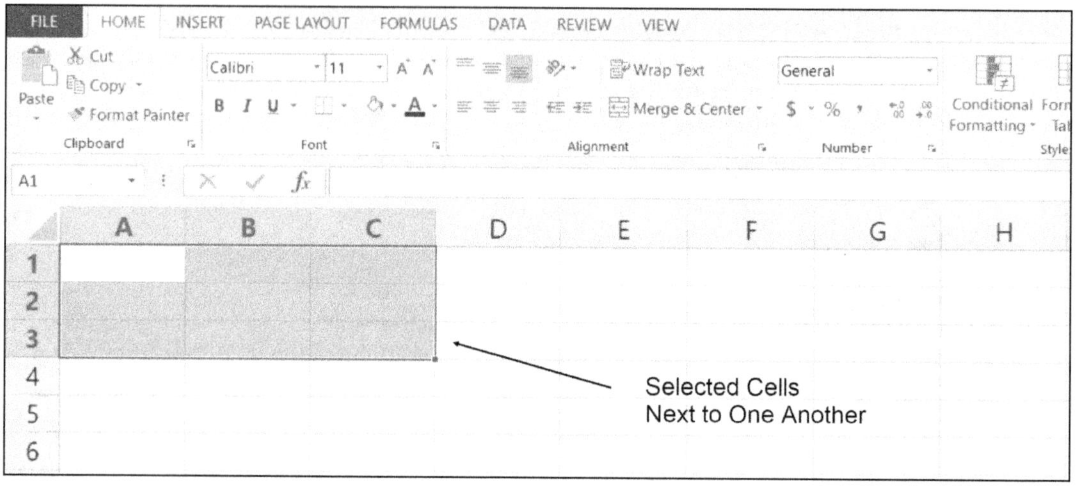

If the cells aren't next to each other, then what you do is left-click on the first cell, hold down the Ctrl key (bottom left of my keyboard), left-click on the next cell, hold down the Ctrl key, left-click on the next cell, etc. until you've selected all the cells you want. The cells you've already selected will be shaded in gray and the one you selected last will be surrounded by a dark border that is not as dark as the normal border you see when you just select one cell. In the image below cells A1, C1, A3, and C3 are selected.

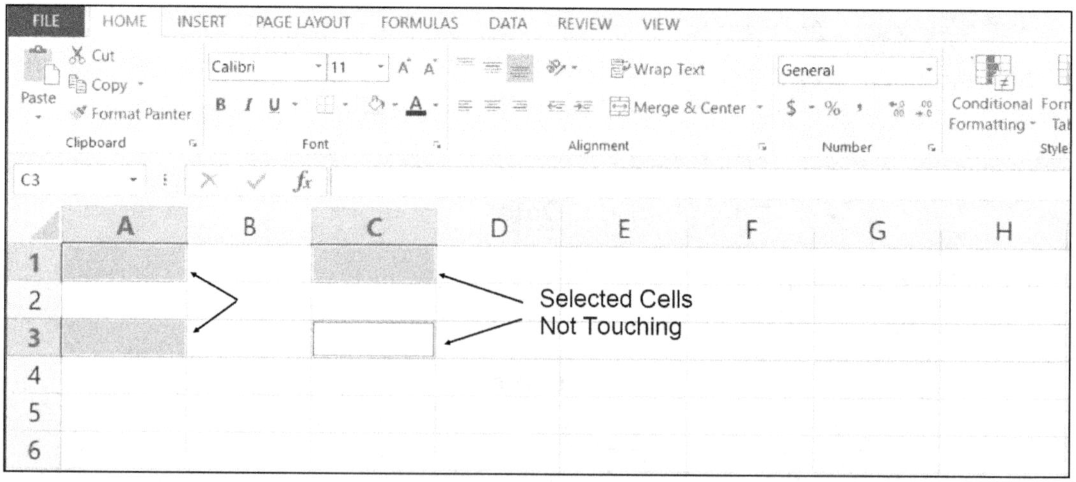

Dropdown

I will occasionally refer to a dropdown or dropdown menu. This is generally a list of potential choices that you can select from. The existence of the list is indicated by an arrow next to the first available selection.

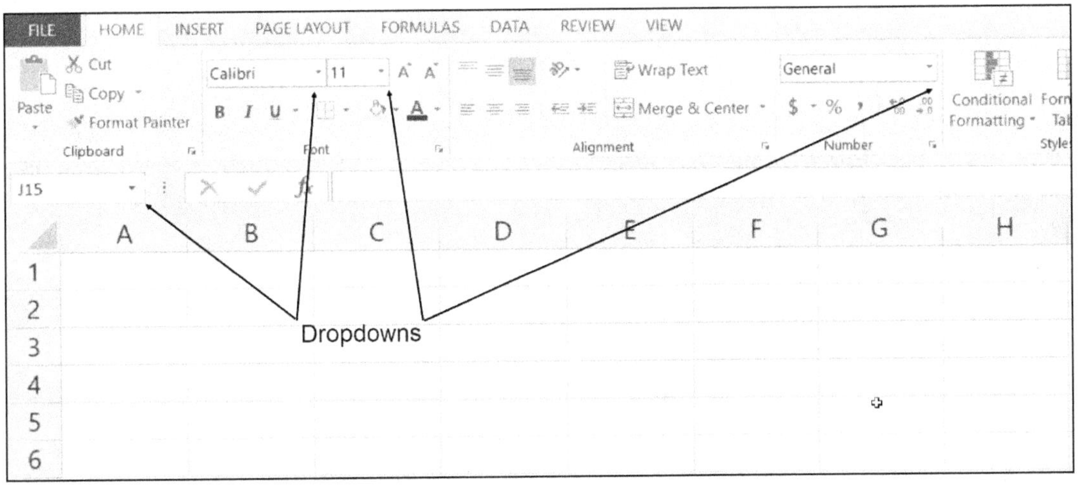

I will also sometimes refer to the list of options you see when you click on a dropdown arrow as the dropdown menu.

Dialogue Box

Dialogue boxes are pop-up boxes that contain a set of available options and appear when you need to provide additional information or make additional choices. For example, this is the Insert dialogue box that appears when you choose to insert a cell:

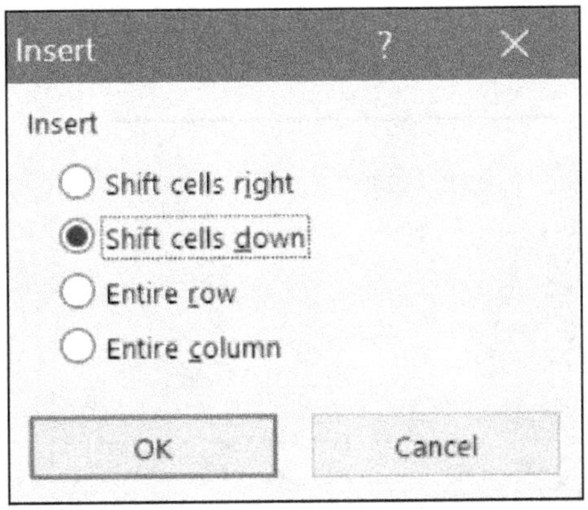

Cursor

If you didn't know this one already, it's what moves around when you move the mouse (or use the trackpad). In Excel it often looks like a three-dimensional squat cross or it will look like one of a couple of varieties of arrow. (Open Excel and move it to where the column and row labels are to see what I mean.) The different shapes the cursor takes represent different functions.

Arrow

If I say that you can "arrow" to something that just means to use the arrow keys to navigate from one cell to another. For example, if you enter information in A1 and hit enter, that moves your cursor down to cell A2. If instead you wanted to move to Cell B1, you could do so with the right arrow.

ABSOLUTE BASICS

It occurs to me that there are a few absolute basics to using Excel that we should cover before we get into things like formatting.

Opening an Excel File

To start a brand new Excel file, I simply click on Excel 2013 from my applications menu or the shortcut I have on my computer's taskbar, and it opens a new Excel file for me.

If you're opening an existing Excel file, you can either go to the folder where the file is saved and double-click on the file name, or you can (if Excel is already open) go to the File tab and choose Open from the left-hand menu.

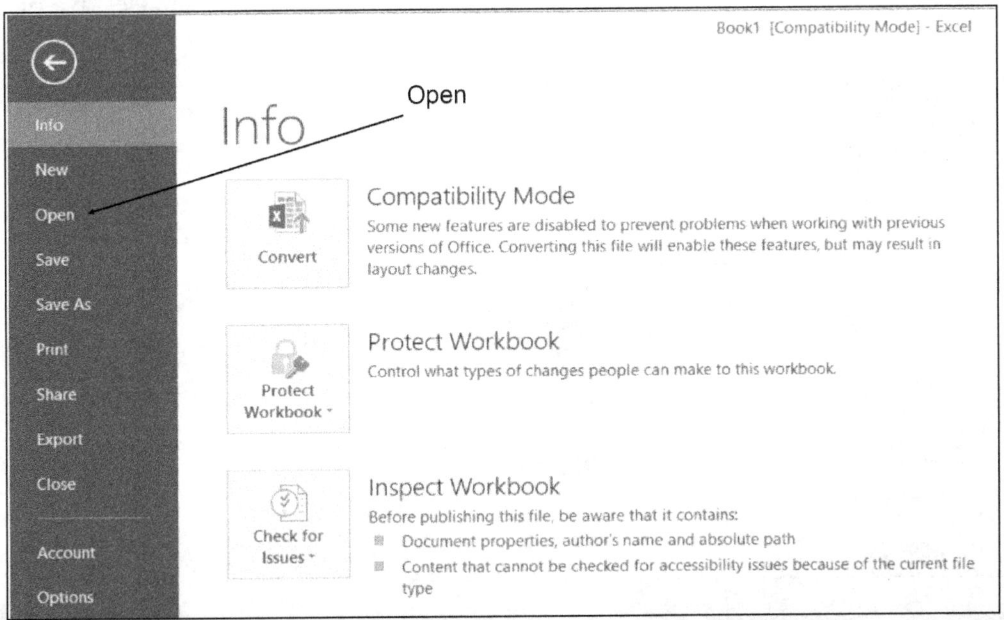

That will show you a list of Recent Workbooks. If it includes the one you're looking for, you can just click on it once and it will open.

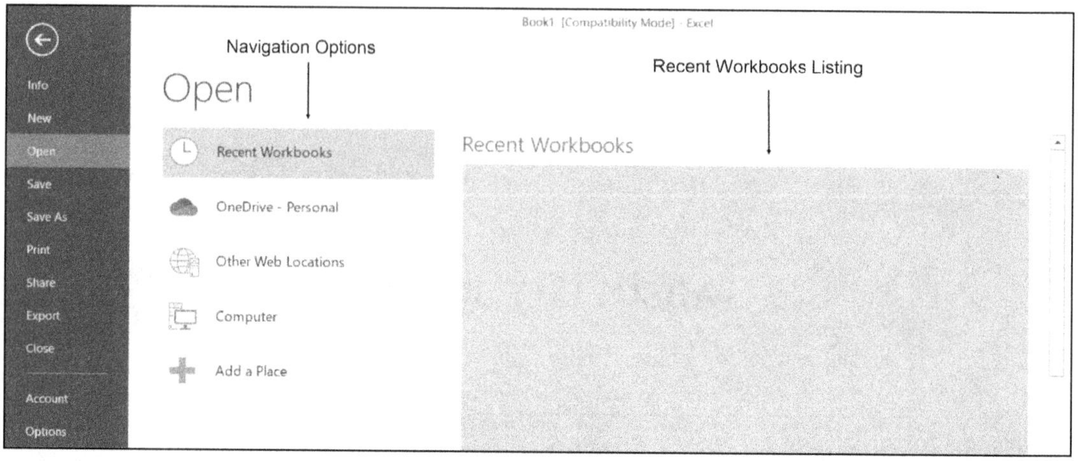

If you don't see the file you're looking for, you can click on the list of navigation options in between the left-hand menu and the list of Recent Workbooks and navigate to where the file is stored. When I click on Computer it gives me the current folder I'm in as well as five recent folders and an option to browse if the folder I want isn't one of the ones displayed.

Saving an Excel File

To save a file you can go to the File tab at the top of the screen and then choose Save or Save As from the menu options on the left side.

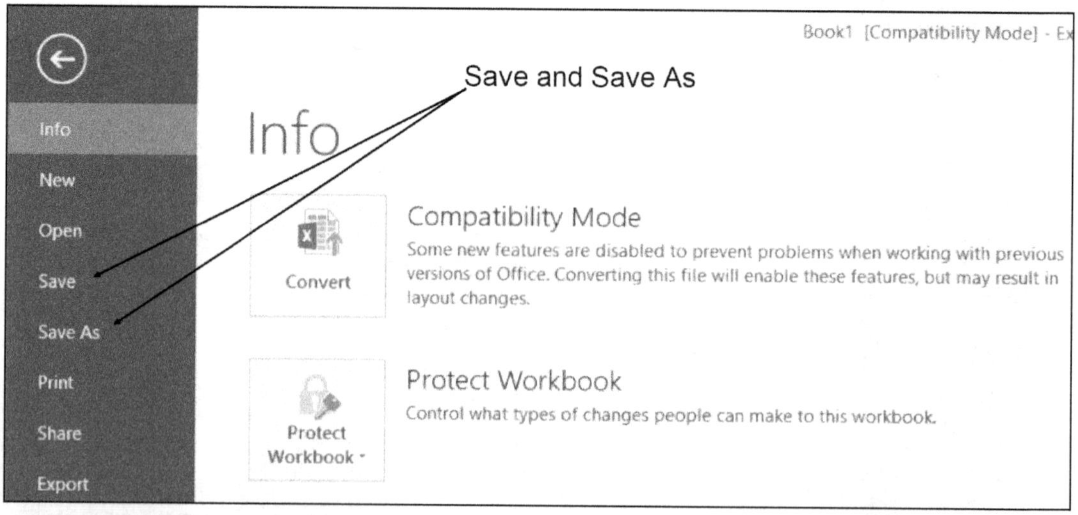

When you're dealing with a new Excel file, you really only have the Save As option. (When I click on Save it still takes me to Save As.) With Save As, Excel will ask you to choose which folder to save the file into. You can either choose from the list of recent folders on the right-hand side or navigate to the folder you want using the locations listing on the left of that list.

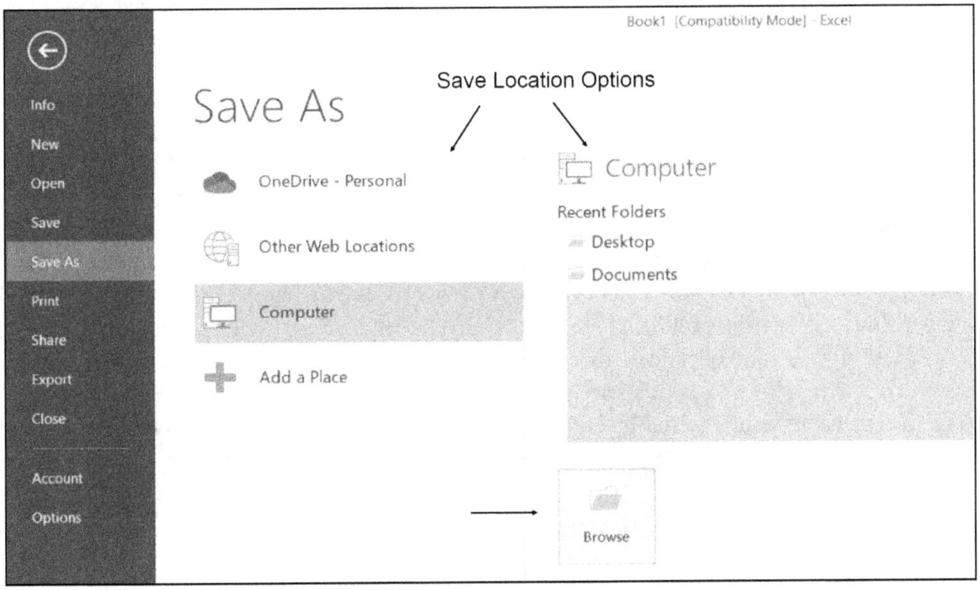

Once you choose a location, a dialogue box will appear where you can name the file.

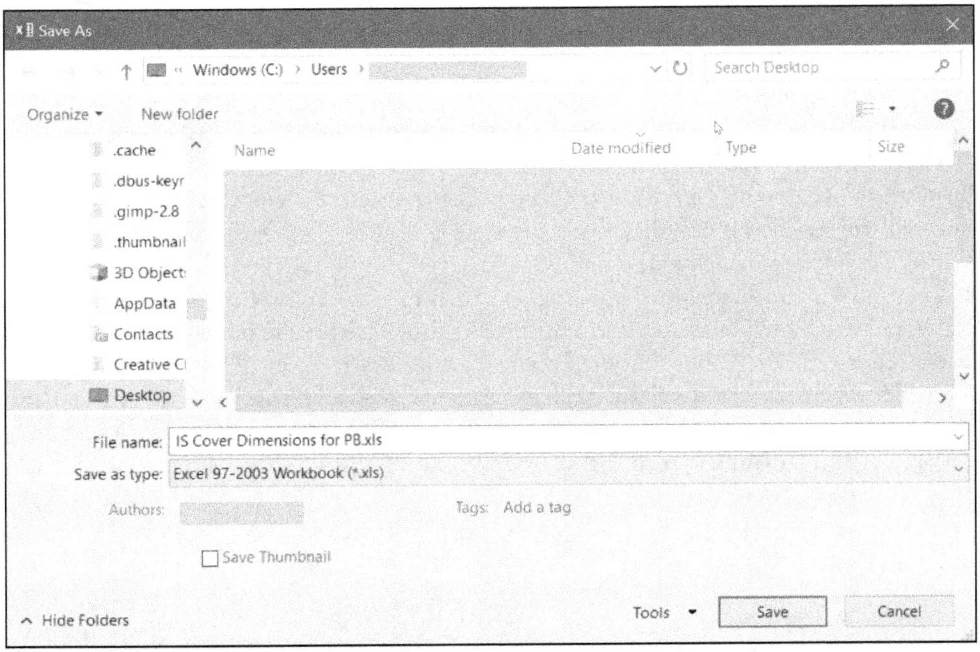

My save options default to an .xls file type. I don't know if this is standard or if I've set it up that way somewhere. If yours doesn't default to the .xls file type, I'd recommend using that file type as much as possible if you think you might share the file at any point. The newer versions of Excel actually are an .xlsx file type, but if you use that file type and want to share with someone who has a version of Excel that's pre-2007, they won't be able to open your file.

It's much easier to save down to an older version than have to convert up to a newer version. And I'm pretty sure if you're using this guide you won't be using any of the fancy options that are available in the newest versions of Excel that aren't available in older versions. If it turns out you are, Excel will generate a warning message about compatibility when you save the file as an .xls file, and you can decide not to save it to the older version at that time.

If you're saving a file you've already saved once before and you have no changes to its name, location, or type, you can go to File>Save and it will save it for you, keeping all of that information the same. You can also just type Ctrl and S at the same time (Ctrl+S) (Note: Even though I'm going to show these commands with a capital letter, you don't have to use the capitalized version of the letter.)

Or, and I think this is true of all Excel users, there should be a small computer disk image in the top left corner that you can click on. (You can customize that list and I have for my most-used functions, which is why I'm not 100% sure.)

If you're saving a file you've already saved once before but you want to save it to a new location, change its name, or change the file type (.xls to .xlsx, for example), use Save As.

Deleting an Excel File

You can't delete an Excel file from within Excel. You'll need to navigate to the folder where the file is stored and delete the file there without opening it. First, click on the file name. (Only enough to select it. Make sure you haven't double-clicked and highlighted the name which will then try to rename the file.) Next, choose Delete from the menu at the top of the screen, or right-click and choose Delete from the dropdown menu.

Renaming an Excel File

You might want to rename an Excel file at some point. You can Save As and choose a new name for the file, but that will mean you now have two versions of the file, one with the old name and one with the new name. Or you can navigate to where you've saved the file, click on it once to highlight the file, click on it a second time to highlight the name, and then type in the new name you want to use. If you do it that way, there will only be one version of the file, the one with the name you wanted.

If you do rename a file, know that you can't then access it from the Recent Workbooks listing under Open file. Even though it might be listed there, Excel won't be able to find it because it no longer has that name. (Same thing happens if you move a file from the location it was in when you were last working on it. I often run into this by moving a file into a new subfolder when I suddenly get inspired to organize my records.)

NAVIGATING EXCEL

The next thing we're going to discuss is basic navigation within Excel. These are all things you can do that don't involve inputting, formatting, or manipulating your data.

Basic Navigation Within A Worksheet

Excel will automatically open into cell A1 of Sheet 1 for a new Excel file. For an existing file it will open in the cell and worksheet where you were when you last saved the file. (This means it can also open with a set of cells already highlighted if that's what you were doing when you last saved the file.)

Within a worksheet, it's pretty basic to navigate.

You can click into any cell you can see in the worksheet with your mouse or trackpad. Just place your cursor over the cell and left-click.

From the cell where you currently are (which will be outlined with a dark border), you can use the up, down, left, and right arrow keys to move one cell in any of those directions.

You can also use the tab key to move one cell to the right and the shift and tab keys combined (shift + tab) to move one cell to the left.

To see other cells in the worksheet that aren't currently visible, you can use the scroll bars on the right-hand side or the bottom of the worksheet. The right-hand-side scroll bar will let you move up and down. The bottom scroll bar will let you move right or left. Just remember that the bars themselves will only let you move as far as you've entered data, you need to use the arrows at the ends of the scroll bars to move farther than that.

For worksheets with lots of data in them, click on the scroll bar and drag it to move quickly to the beginning or end of the data. To move one view's worth at a time, click in the blank space around the actual bar.

If you're using the scroll bars to navigate, remember that until you click into a new cell with your mouse or trackpad you will still be in the last cell where you clicked or made an edit. (You can test this by typing and you'll see that you're brought back to that last cell, wherever it is.)

Basic Navigation Between Worksheets

Between worksheets, you can either click on the name of the worksheet you want (at the bottom of the screen) or you can use Ctrl and Page Up (Ctrl + Page Up) to move one worksheet to the left and Ctrl and Page Down (Ctrl + Page Dn) to move one worksheet to the right.

F2

If you click in a cell and hit the F2 key, this will take you to the end of the contents of the cell. This can be very useful when you need to edit the contents of a cell or to work with a formula in that cell.

Insert a Cell in a Worksheet

(See the next section for how to insert an entire row or column.) Sometimes you just want to insert one cell in the worksheet. To do so, click on where you want to insert the cell, right-click, and select Insert.

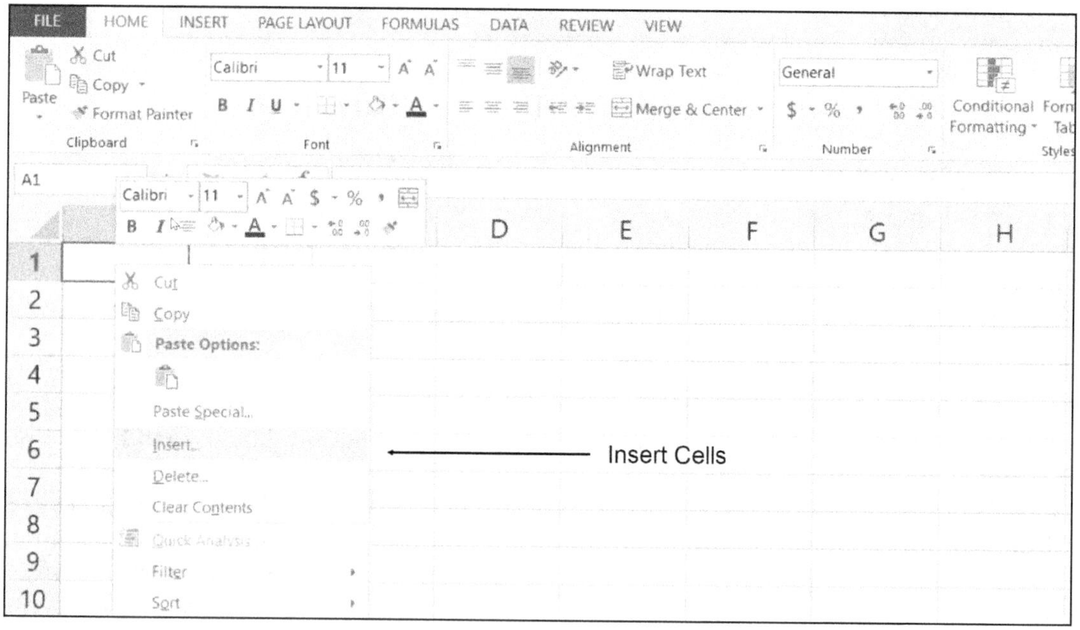

You'll be given four choices, Shift Cells Right, Shift Cells Down, Entire Row, and Entire Column.

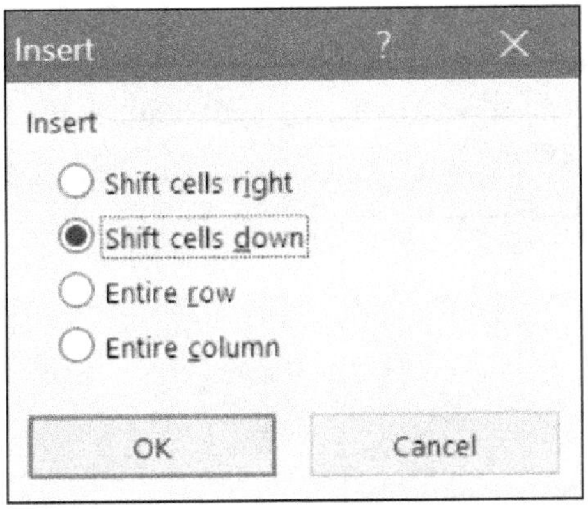

Shift Cells Right will insert your cell by moving every other cell in that row to the right. Shift Cells Down will insert your cell by moving every other cell in that column down. Entire row will insert an entire row instead of one cell. Entire column will insert an entire column instead of one cell.

Be sure that the option you choose makes sense given the other data you've already entered in the worksheet. Sometimes I find that I need to actually highlight a group of cells and insert cells for all of them to keep the rest of my cells aligned.

You can also highlight the cell(s) where you want to insert cell(s) and then go to the Cells section of the Home tab where it says Insert. Choose the insert option you want from there, the same way you would for inserting a worksheet.

Insert a Column or Row

Sometimes you'll enter information and then realize that you want to add an entire row or column right in the midst of the data you've already entered. If this happens, highlight the row or column where you want your new row or column to go, right-click, and select Insert. (By highlight, I mean click on either the letter of the column or the number of the row to select the entire column or row.) Your data will either shift one entire column to the right or one entire row downward, starting with the column or row you selected.

You can also just click in one cell and then choose Entire Row or Entire Column after right-clicking and choosing Insert.

Another option is to highlight the row or column and then go to the Cells section of the Home tab where it says Insert and choose the insert option you want from there.

Insert a New Worksheet

When you open a new Excel file, you'll have one worksheet you can use named Sheet 1. (In Excel 2007 I had three worksheets available when I opened a new file.)

If you need another worksheet, simply click on the + symbol in a circle at the end of your existing worksheets to add a new one. (In Excel 2007 the add a worksheet option looked like a mini worksheet with a yellow star in the corner.)

You can also go to the Home tab under the Cells section and left-click the arrow under Insert then select Insert Sheet from the dropdown menu.

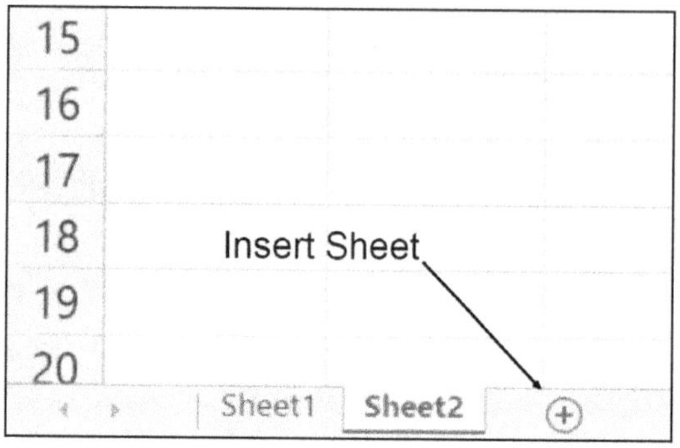

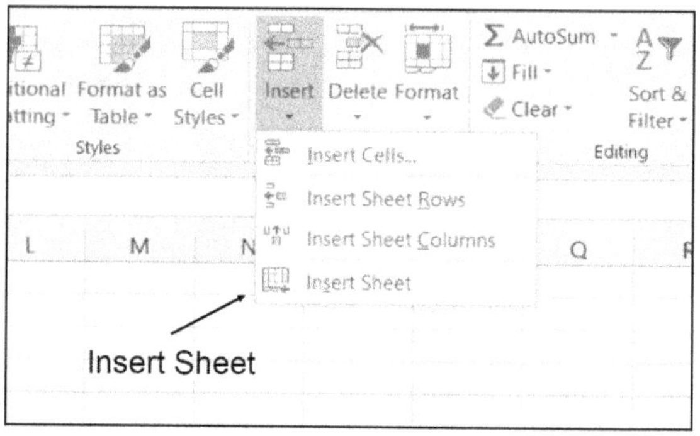

Delete a Cell in a Worksheet

Deleting a cell in a worksheet is a lot like inserting a cell. Right-click on the cell you want to delete and choose Delete from the dropdown menu. Next choose whether to shift cells up or left. (When you remove a cell everything will have to move to fill in the empty space it leaves.) Be sure that deleting that one cell doesn't change the layout of the rest of your data. As with inserting a cell, I sometimes find I need to delete more than one cell to keep things uniform in my presentation.

(Note that you can also delete an entire row or column this way as well.)

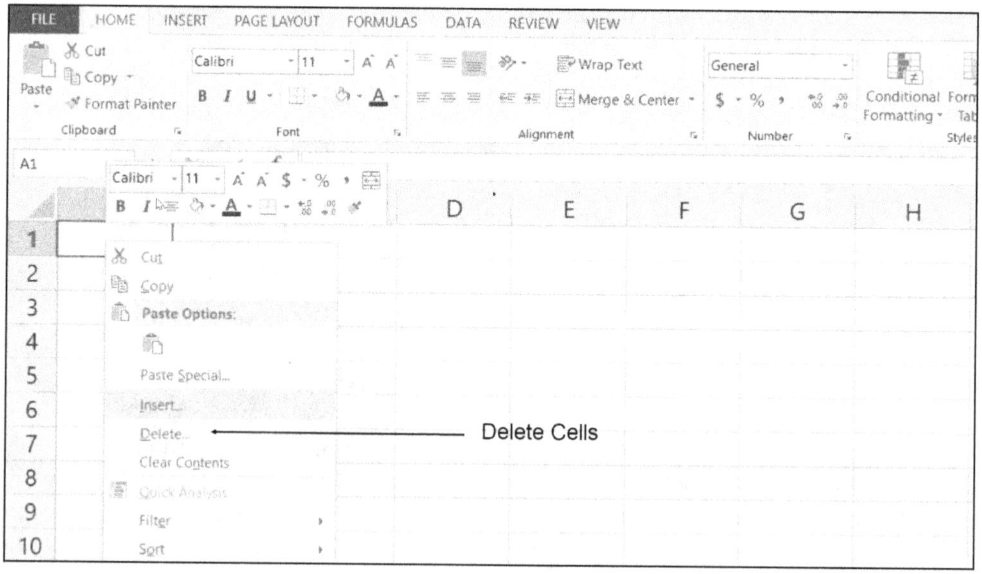

Another option is to highlight the cell(s) you want to delete, and then go to the Cells section of the Home tab where it says Delete and choose the delete option you want from there.

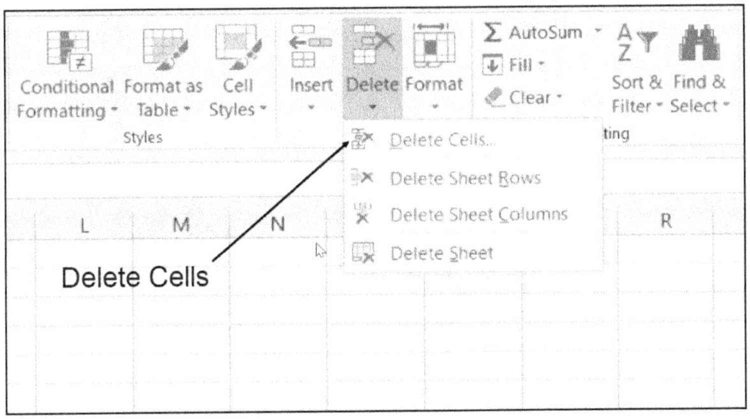

Delete a Column or Row

Highlight the entire row or column you want to delete, right-click, and select Delete. It will automatically delete the row or column. You can also highlight the row or column and then go to the Cells section of the Home tab where it says Delete and choose the delete option you want from there. And, as with inserting a row or column, you can click into one cell, right-click, select Delete, and then choose Entire Row or Entire Column from the dialogue box.

Delete a Worksheet

Sometimes you'll add a worksheet and then realize you don't want it anymore. It's easy enough to delete. Just right-click on the name of the worksheet you want to delete and choose the Delete option from the dropdown menu.

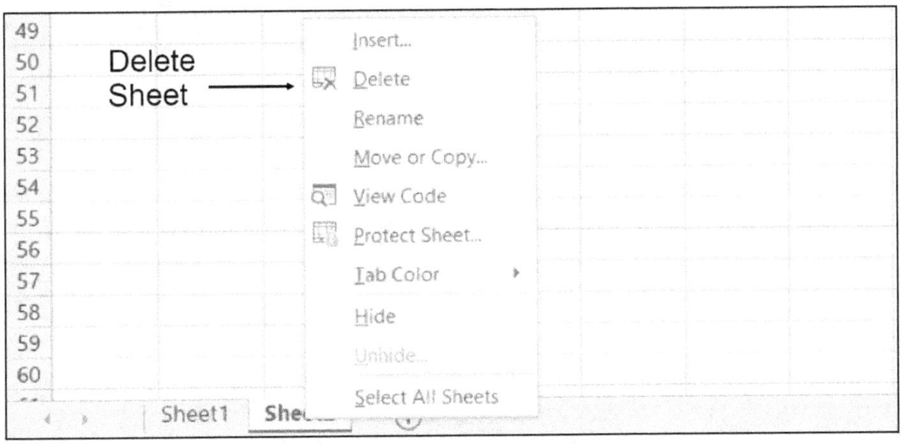

You can also go to the Cells section in the Home tab, left-click on the arrow under Delete, and choose Delete Sheet from the dropdown menu.

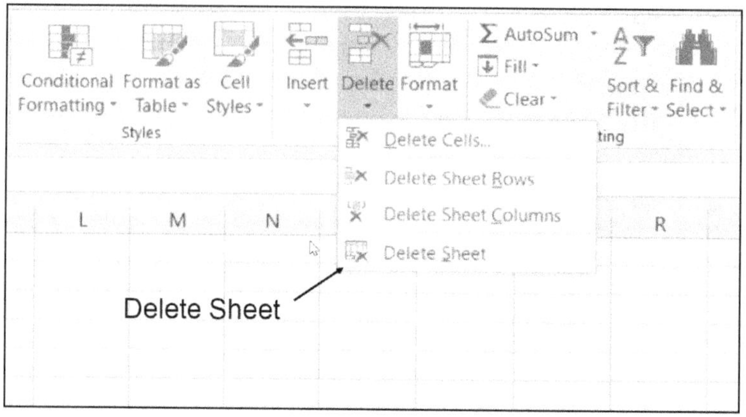

If there was any data in the worksheet you're trying to delete, it will give you a warning message to that effect. If you don't care, click Delete. If you didn't realize there was data and want to cancel the deletion, click Cancel.

Be sure you want to delete any worksheet you choose to delete, because you can't get it back later. This is one place where undo will not work.

Rename A Worksheet

The default name for worksheets in Excel are Sheet 1, Sheet 2, Sheet 3, etc. They're not useful for much of anything, and if you have information in more than one worksheet, you're going to want to rename them to something that lets you identify which worksheet is which.

If you double left-click on a worksheet name (on the tab at the bottom) it will highlight in gray and you can then delete the existing name and replace it with whatever you want.

You can also right-click on the tab name and choose Rename from the dropdown menu.

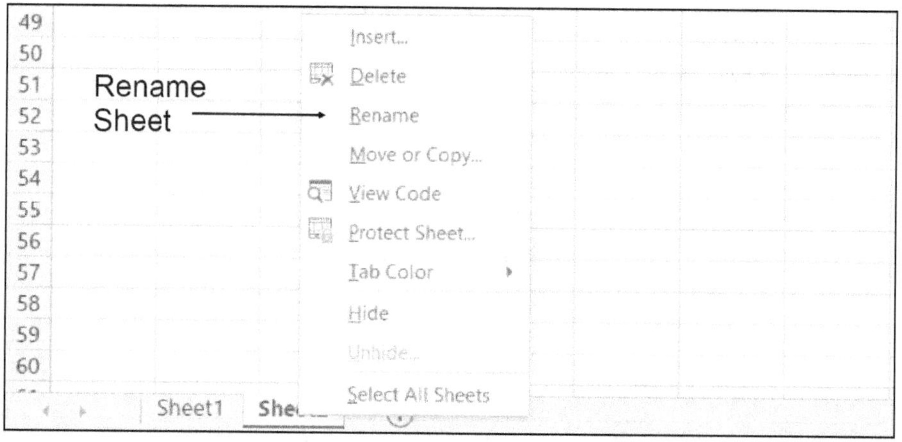

A worksheet name cannot be more than 31 characters long, be blank, contain the forward slash, the back slash, a question mark, a star, a colon, or brackets (/ \ ? * : [ ]), begin or end with an apostrophe, or be named History. Don't worry. In my version of Excel it just stops you from typing those characters or past the limit. (In earlier versions I believe it let you type the incorrect characters and then gave an error message and refused to accept the name.)

INPUTTING YOUR DATA

At its most basic, inputting your data is very simple. Click in the cell where you want to input information and type. But there are some tricks to it that you'll want to keep in mind.

First, let's take a step back and talk about one of the key strengths of a using Excel and that's the ability to sort or filter your data. For example, I self-publish books, and every month I get reports from the places where my books are published listing all of the sales of my books at those locations. But what if I only care about the sales of book A? How can I see those if I have a couple hundred rows of information in the report they've given me?

Well, if the site where I sold those books is nice and helpful and they understand data analysis, they've given me my sales listings in an Excel worksheet with one header row at the top and then one row for each sale or each book. If they've done that, then I can very easily filter my data on the title column and see just the entries related to title A. If they haven't, then I'm stuck deleting rows of information I don't need to get to the data I want.

Which is all a roundabout way of saying that you can input your data any way you want, but if you follow some key data principles you'll have a lot more flexibility in what you can do with your data once it's entered.

Those principles are:

1. Use the first row of your worksheet to label your data.
2. List all of your data in continuous rows after that first row without including any subtotals or subheadings or anything that isn't your data.
3. To the extent possible, format your data in such a way that it can be analyzed. (So rather than put in a free-text field, try to use a standardized list of values instead. See below. Column E, which uses a 1 to 5 point ranking scale, is better for analysis than Column D, which is a free text field where anyone can say anything.)
4. Standardize your values. Customer A should always be listed as Customer A. United States should always be United States not USA, U.S.A., or America.
5. Store your raw data in one location; analyze or correct it elsewhere.

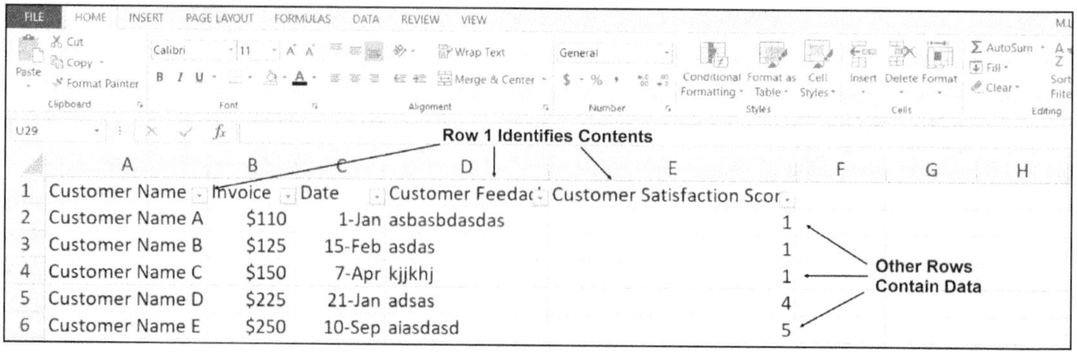

Now, I'm saying all of this, but some of the ways I use Excel don't conform to these principles. And that's fine. My budgeting worksheet is not meant to be filtered or sorted. It's a snapshot of information that summarizes my current financial position. But my worksheet that lists all vendor payments for the year? You bet it's formatted using this approach.

So before you enter any data into your Excel file, put some time into thinking about how you want to use that data. Is it just a visual snapshot? If so, don't worry about structuring it for sorting or filtering. Will it be hundreds of rows of values that you want to summarize or analyze? If so, then arrange it the way I listed above. You don't have to have row 1 be your column headings, but wherever you put those headings, keep everything below that point single rows of data that are all formatted and entered using the same definitions.

Okay. So what are some tricks to make entering your information easier?

Undo

If you enter the wrong information or perform the wrong action and want to easily undo it, hold down the Ctrl key and the Z key at the same time. (Ctrl + Z) You can do this multiple times if you want to undo multiple actions, although there are a few actions (such as deleting a worksheet) that cannot be undone.

Redo

If you mistakenly undo something and want it back, you can hold down the Ctrl key and the Y key at the same time to redo it. (Ctrl + Y)

Auto-Suggested Text

If you've already typed text into a cell, Excel will suggest that text to you in subsequent cells in the same column.

For example, if you are creating a list of all the books you own (something I once tried to do and gave up after about a hundred entries), and in cell A1 you type "science fiction", when you go to cell A2 and type an "s", Excel will automatically suggest to you "science fiction". If you don't want to use that suggestion, then keep typing. If you do, then hit enter.

Nice, huh? Instead of typing fifteen characters you were able to type one.

This only works when you have unique values for Excel to identify. If you have science fiction/fantasy and science fiction as entries in that column, it's not going to work. Excel waits until it can suggest one option, so you'd have to type science fiction/ before it made any suggestions.

Also, if there are empty cells between the entries you already completed and the one you're now completing and you have no other columns with completed data in them that bridge that gap, Excel won't make a suggestion.

Another time it doesn't work is if you have a very long list that you've completed and the matching entry is hundreds of rows away from the one you're now completing.

Excel also doesn't make suggestions for numbers. And if you have an entry that combines letters and numbers, it won't make a suggestion until you've typed at least one letter.

Despite all these apparent limitations, auto-suggested text can be very handy to use if you have to enter one of a limited number of choices over and over again and can't easily copy the information into your worksheet.

Copying the Contents and Formatting of One Cell To Another

This is very easy. Highlight the information you want to copy and hold down the Ctrl and C keys at the same time (Ctrl + C). Go to the cell where you want to put the information you copied and hit Enter.

If you want to copy to more than one location, instead of hitting Enter at the new cell, hold down the Ctrl and V keys at the same time (Ctrl + V). If you use Ctrl + V, you'll see that the original cell you copied from is still surrounded by a dotted line meaning that text is still available to be pasted into another cell.

You can also right-click and select Copy from the dropdown menu and then right-click Paste from the dropdown menu in the cell where you want the information. (In my version of Excel, right-click Paste is now represented by a clipboard with a plain white page under the Paste Options header.)

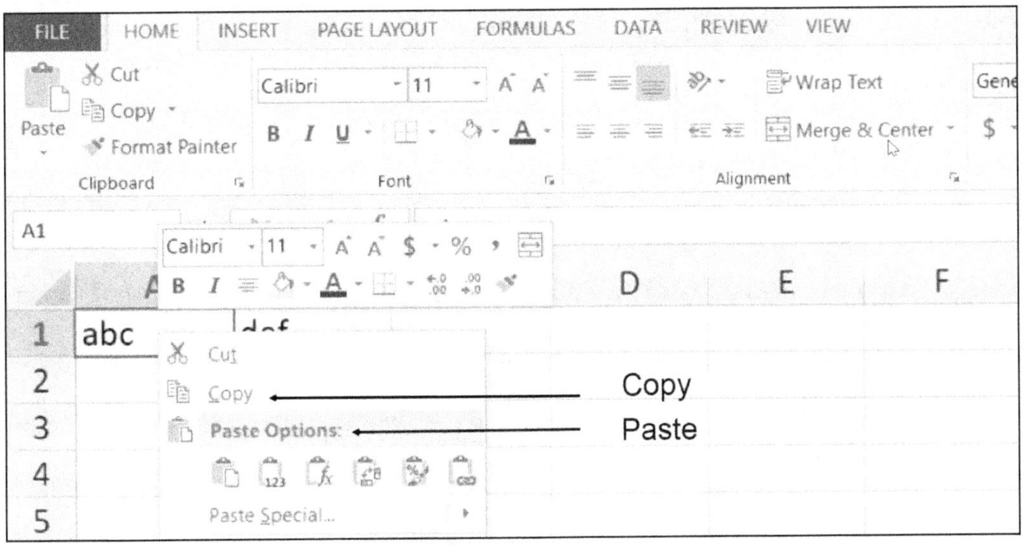

Once you're done pasting the values into new cells and want to do something else, just hit the Esc key. This will remove the dotted line from around the cell you were copying and ensure you don't accidentally paste it somewhere else. Typing in a new cell also works.

Moving the Contents of a Cell (Cutting)

To move the contents of a cell rather than copy it, you select the cell with the contents you want to move, type Ctrl and X at the same time (Ctrl + X), click on the new location, and hit Enter or type Ctrl + V. Unlike with copying, you can only move the contents of a cell to one new location.

Another option is to highlight the cell(s) you want to move, right-click, and choose Cut from the dropdown menu and then paste your cell contents in the new location.

Copying the contents of a cell (Ctrl + C) is different from cutting and moving the contents of a cell (Ctrl + X), because when you copy the contents of a cell they remain in their original location. When you move the contents, you are removing them from their original location to place them in their new location.

Copying Versus Moving When It Comes to Formulas

If you're dealing with text, copying (Ctrl + C) or cutting the text (Ctrl + X) doesn't really change anything. What ends up in that new cell will be the same regardless of the method you use.

But with formulas, that's not what happens.

With formulas, moving the contents of a cell (Ctrl + X) will keep the formula the exact same as it was. So if you're formula was =A2+B2 it will still be =A2+B2 in the new cell.

Copying the contents of a cell (Ctrl + C) will *change the formula* based upon the number of rows and columns you moved. The formula is copied relative to where it originated. If your original formula in cell A3 was =A2+B2 and you copied it to cell A4 (so moved one cell downward) the formula in cell A4 will be =A3+B3. All cell references in the formula will adjust one cell downward.

If you copy that same formula to cell B3 (so one cell to the right) the formula in B3 will be =B2+C2. All cell references in the formula will adjust one cell to the right.

If this doesn't make sense to you, just try it. Put some sample values in cells A2 and B2 and then experiment with Ctrl + C versus Ctrl + X.

Also, there is a way to prevent a formula from changing when you copy it using the $ sign to fix the cell reference. We'll talk about that next.

Copying Formulas To Other Cells While Keeping One Value Fixed

If you want to copy a formula while keeping the value of one or more of the cells fixed, you need to use the $ sign.

A $ sign in front of the letter portion of a cell location will keep the column the same but allow the row number to change. ($A1)

A $ sign in front of the number portion of a cell location will keep the row the same but allow the column to change. (A$1)

A $ sign in front of both will keep the referenced cell exactly the same. (A1)

This is discussed in more detail in the manipulating data section.

Paste Special

Sometimes you want to copy just the contents of a cell without keeping any of its formatting. Or you want to take a list of values in a column and put them into a single row instead.

That's where the Paste Special options come in handy.

First, know that you can only use Paste Special options if you've copied the contents of a cell (Ctrl + C). They don't work if you've cut the contents using Ctrl +X.

To Paste Special, instead of just typing Ctrl + V to paste what you copied into a new cell, right-click in the new cell and choose from the Paste Options section.

You should see in the dropdown menu something like this. What you see will be determined by what you've copied and how.

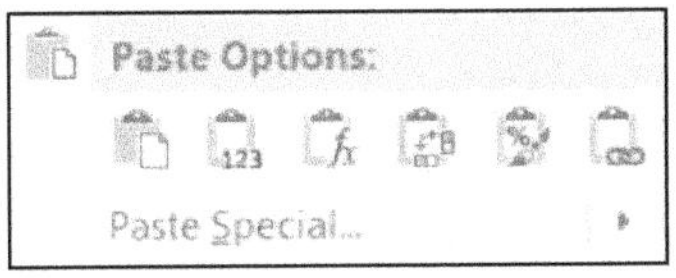

In my opinion, not all of these choices are useful. So I'm just going to highlight two of them for you.

Paste Values, which has the 123 on its clipboard, is useful for when you want the results of a formula, but don't want the formula anymore. I use this often.

It's also useful when you want the contents of a cell, but would prefer to use the formatting from the destination cell(s). For example, if you're copying from one Excel file to another.

Another way I use it is when I've run a set of calculations on my data, found my values, and now want to sort or do something else with my data and don't want to risk having the values change on me. I highlight the entire data set, copy, and then paste special-values right over the top of my existing data. (Just be sure to type Esc after you do this so that the change is fixed in place.)

The Paste Transpose option—the one with the little arrow arcing between two pairs of cells, fourth from the left above—is very useful if you have a row of data that you want to turn into columns of data or vice versa. Just highlight the data, copy, paste-transpose, and it will automatically paste a column of data as a row or a row of data as a column. Just be sure before you paste that there isn't any data already there that will be overwritten, because Excel won't warn you before it overwrites it.

There are more paste options available than just the six you can see above. Click on where it says Paste Special and you'll see another dropdown menu to the side with eight more options, and if you go to the bottom of that breakout menu and click on Paste Special again, it will bring up the Paste Special dialogue box:

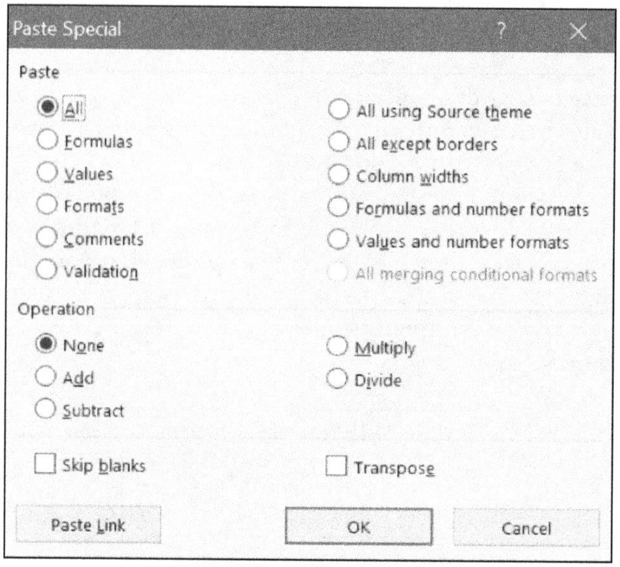

Displaying The Contents Of A Cell As Text

Excel likes to change certain values to what it thinks you meant. So if you enter June 2015 into a cell, it will convert that entry to a date even if you intended it to be text.

It also assumes that any entry that starts with a minus sign (-), an equals sign (=), or a plus sign (+) is a formula.

To keep Excel from doing this, you can type a single quote mark (') before the contents of the cell. If you do that, Excel will treat whatever you enter after that as text and will keep the formatting type as General.

So if you want to have June 2015 display in a cell in your worksheet, you need to type 'June 2015.

If you want to have

- Item A

display in a cell, you need to type it as:

'- Item A

The single quote mark is not visible when you look at or print your worksheet. It is only visible in the formula bar when you've selected that cell.

Entering a Formula Into a Cell

The discussion just above about displaying the contents of a cell as text brings up another good point. If you want Excel to treat an entry as a formula then you need to enter the equals (=), plus (+), or negative sign (-) as your first character in the cell.

So, if you type

1+1

in a cell, that will just display as text in the cell. You'll see

1+1.

But if you type

+1+1

in a cell, Excel will treat that as a formula and calculate it. You'll see

2

in the cell and

=1+1

in the formula bar. Same with if you type

=1+1

It will calculate that as a formula, display 2 in the cell, and show =1+1 in the formula bar. If you type

-1+1

in a cell it will treat that as a formula adding negative 1 to 1 and will show that as 0 in the cell and display

=-1+1

in the formula bar. Best practice is to just use the equals sign to start every formula.

Including Line Breaks Within a Cell

I sometimes need to have multiple lines of text or numbers within a cell. So instead of a, b, c, I need

a
b
c

You can't just hit Enter, because if you do it'll take you to the next cell. Instead, hold down the Alt key at the same time you hit Enter. This will create a line break within the cell.

Deleting Data

If you enter information into a cell and later decide you want to delete it, you can click on that cell(s) and use the delete button on your computer's keyboard. This will remove whatever you entered in the cell without deleting the cell as well.

You can also double-click into the cell or use F2 to get to the end of the contents and then use your computer's backspace key to delete out the contents of the cell.

Deleting the contents of a cell will not remove its formatting. To delete the contents of a cell as well as its formatting, go to the Editing section of the Home tab, click on the dropdown next to the Clear option, and choose to Clear All.

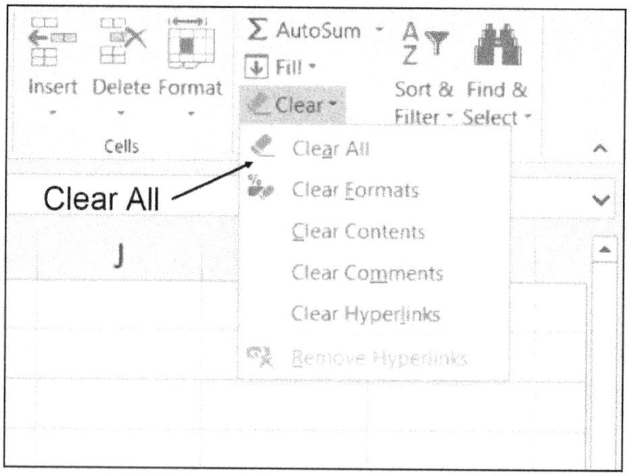

Find and Replace

Sometimes you have a big worksheet and you need to find a specific entry. An easy way to do this is to use the Find option. The easiest way to access it is to type Ctrl and F at the same time (Ctrl + F). This opens the Find dialogue box. Type what you're looking for into the "Find what" field and hit enter. The default is for find to look in formulas as well, so if you search for "f" and have a formula that references cell F11, it will hit on that as much as it will hit on the cell that actually contains the letter f in a word.

You can change this setting under Options.

The other way to access Find is through the Editing section of the Home tab. The Find & Select option has a dropdown menu that includes Find.

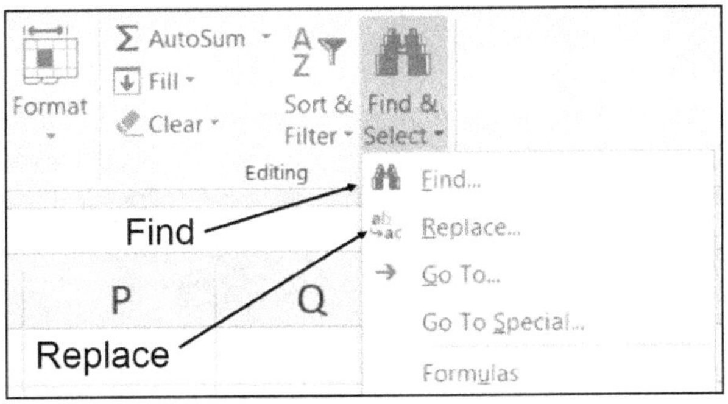

If you're looking for something in order to change it, you can use Replace instead. Type Ctrl and H (Ctrl + H) at the same time (or just Ctrl + F and then click over to the Replace tab), or you can access it through the Editing section of the Home tab.

When the Replace dialogue box opens, you'll see two lines, "Find what" and "Replace with." In the "Find what" line, type what you're looking for. In the "Replace with" line, type what to replace it with.

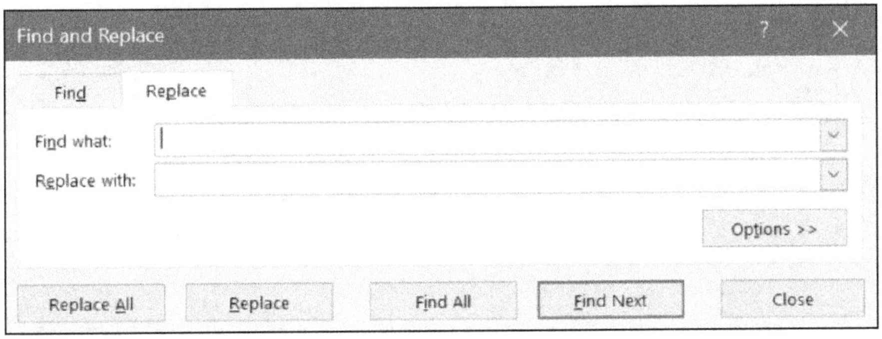

Be VERY careful using Replace. Say you want to replace "hat" with "chapeau" because you've suddenly become pretentious. If you don't think this through, you will end up replacing every usage of hat, even when it's in words like "that" or "chat". So you'll end up with "tchapeau" in the middle of a sentence instead of "that" because the hat portion of that was replaced with chapeau. (This probably happens in Word more than in Excel, but it's still something to be aware of.)

Replace is good for removing something like double spaces or converting formatting of a particular value, but otherwise you might want to use find and then manually correct each entry to avoid inadvertent errors.

Copying Patterns of Data

Sometimes you'll want to input data that repeats itself. Like, for example, the days of the week. Say you're putting together a worksheet that lists the date and what day of the week it is for an entire year. You could type out Monday, Tuesday, Wednesday, Thursday, Friday, Saturday, Sunday, and then copy and paste that 52 times. Or…

You could take advantage of the fact that Excel can recognize patterns. With this particular example, it looks like all it takes is typing in Monday. Do that and then go to the bottom right corner of the cell with Monday in it and position you cursor so that it looks like a small black cross. Left-click, hold that left-click down, and start to drag your cursor away from the cell. Excel should auto-complete the cells below or to the right of the Monday cell with the days of the week in order and repeating themselves in order for as long as you need it to.

If you're dealing with a pattern that isn't as standard as days of the week, sometimes it takes a few rows of data before Excel can identify the pattern. For example, if I type 1 into a cell and try to drag it, Excel just repeats the 1 over and over again. If I do 1 and then 2 and highlight both cells and start to drag from the bottom of the cell with the 2 in it, then it starts to number the next cells 3, 4, 5 etc.

You'll see the values Excel suggests for each cell as you drag the cursor through that cell, but those values won't actually appear in those cells until you're done highlighting all the cells you want to copy the pattern to and you let up on the left-click. (If that doesn't make sense, just try it a few times and you'll see what I mean.)

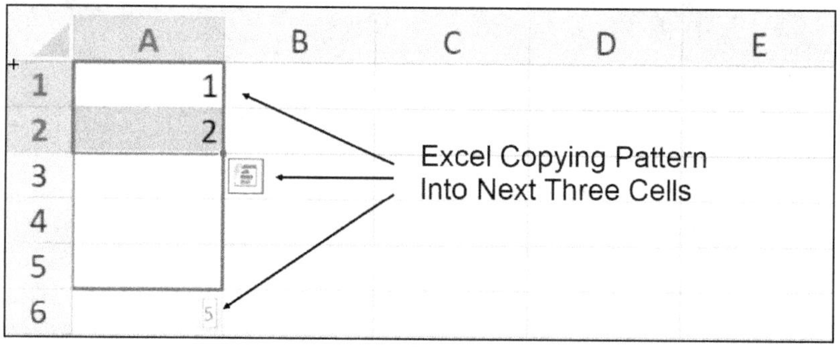

(You can combine Excel's ability to copy patterns with the AutoFill option by double-clicking in the bottom right-hand corner instead. This only works when your current column is next to a column that already has values in it for all of your rows. See the Manipulating Your Data section for more detail on AutoFill.)

Freeze Panes

If you have enough information in a worksheet for it to not be visible in one page, there's a chance you'll want to use freeze panes. What it does is freezes a row or rows and/or a column or columns at the top of your page so that even when you scroll down or to the right those rows or columns stay visible. So if you have 100 rows of information but always want to be able to see your header row, freeze panes will let you do that.

To freeze panes, go to the View tab and click on the arrow under Freeze Panes. It gives you three options: Freeze Panes, Freeze Top Row, and Freeze First Column. Those second two are pretty obvious, right? Choose "Freeze Top Row" and you'll always see Row 1 of your worksheet no matter how far down you scroll. Choose "Freeze First Column" and you'll always see Column A of your worksheet no matter how far to the right you scroll.

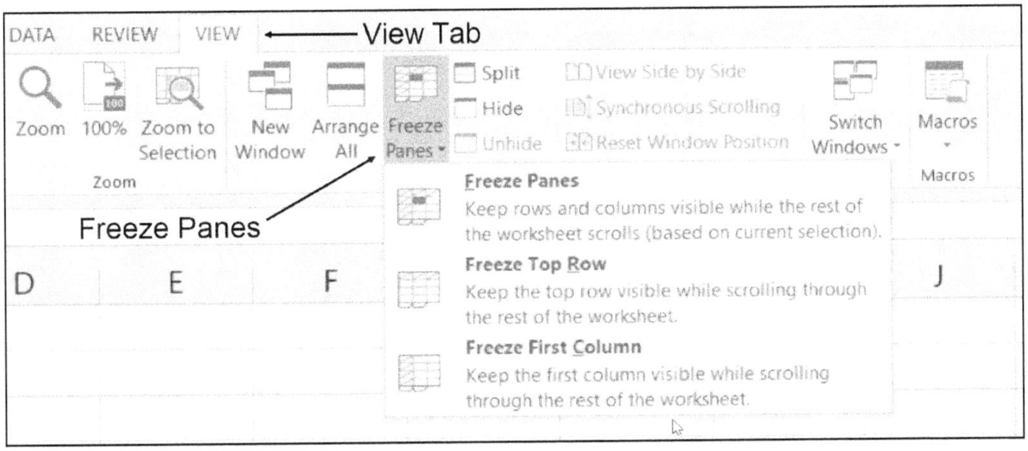

That first option, Freeze Panes, is more interesting. It will freeze as many rows or columns as you need to freeze. If I click on cell C4 (so down three rows and over two columns) and choose to Freeze Panes, it will keep the top three rows and the left two columns of my worksheet visible no matter how far I scroll in the document. So, for example, if you had customer name, city, and state in your first three columns and wanted to be able to see that information as you scrolled over to see other customer data, you could. Or say your worksheet has a couple of rows of text and then the real row labels begin in row 5, you can click in Cell A6, choose to freeze panes, and those top five rows will always stay visible.

Freeze panes is very handy when dealing with large amounts of data. Just be careful that you don't accidentally lose where you are. If you click into a frozen row or column and then arrow down or over, it will take you to the next row, not the data you're seeing on the screen. So if you were looking at row 10,522 and you had the top row frozen and click into row 1 for some reason and then arrow down it will take you to row 2. (It happens to be something I do often, so figured it was worth mentioning.)

To remove freeze panes, you can go back to the View tab and the Freeze Panes dropdown and you'll now see that that first option has become Unfreeze Panes. Just click on it and your document will go back to normal.

FORMATTING

If you're going to spend any amount of time working in Excel then you need to learn how to format cells, because inevitably your column won't be as wide as you want it to be or you'll want to have a cell with red-colored text or to use bolding or italics or something that isn't Excel's default.

That's what this section is for. It's an alphabetical listing of different things you might want to do. You can either format one cell at a time by highlighting that specific cell, or you can format multiple cells at once by highlighting all of them and then choosing your formatting option.

What you'll see below is that there are basically two main ways to format cells. You can use the Home tab and click on the option you want from there, or you can right-click and select the Format Cells option from the dropdown menu. For basic formatting, the Home tab will be the best choice. For less common formatting choices, you may need to use the Format Cells option.

There are also shortcut keys available for things like bolding (Ctrl + B), italicizing (Ctrl + I), and underlining (Ctrl +U) that give a third option for some basic formatting needs.

Aligning Your Text Within a Cell

By default, text within a cell is left-aligned and bottom-aligned. But at times you may want to adjust this. I often will center text or prefer for it to be top-aligned because it looks better to me that way when I have some column headers that are one line and others that are multiple lines.

To do this, highlight the cell(s) you want to change, and go to the Alignment section on the Home tab. You'll see on the left-hand side of that section six different images with lines in them. These are visual representations of your possible choices. The first row has the top aligned, middle aligned, and bottom aligned options. You can choose one of these three options for your cell. The second row has the left-aligned, centered, and right-aligned options. You can also choose one of these three options for your cell. So you can have a cell with top-aligned and centered text or top-aligned and right-aligned text or bottom-aligned and centered text, etc.

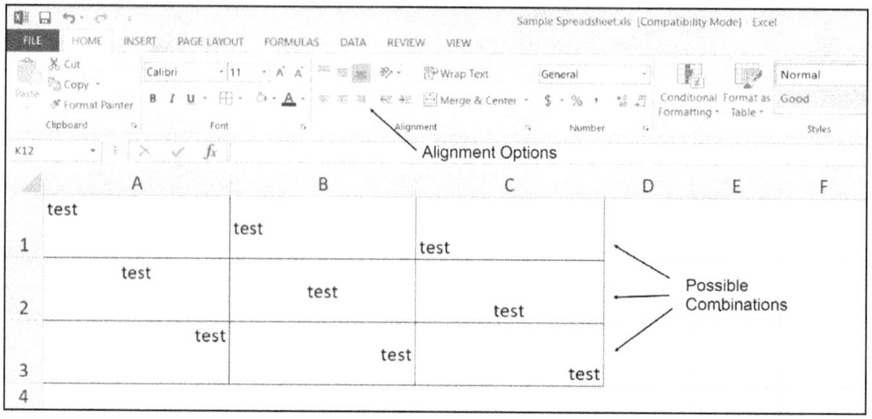

The angled "ab" with an arrow under it on the top row of the Alignment section also has a handful of pre-defined options for changing the direction of text within a cell. You can choose to Angle Counterclockwise, Angle Clockwise, Vertical Text, Rotate Text Up, and Rotate Text Down. (It also offers another way to access the Alignment tab of the Format Cells dialogue box which we'll talk about next. Just click on Format Cell Alignment at the bottom of the dropdown menu.)

Another way to change the text alignment within a cell(s) is to highlight your cell(s) and then right-click and choose Format Cells from the dropdown menu.

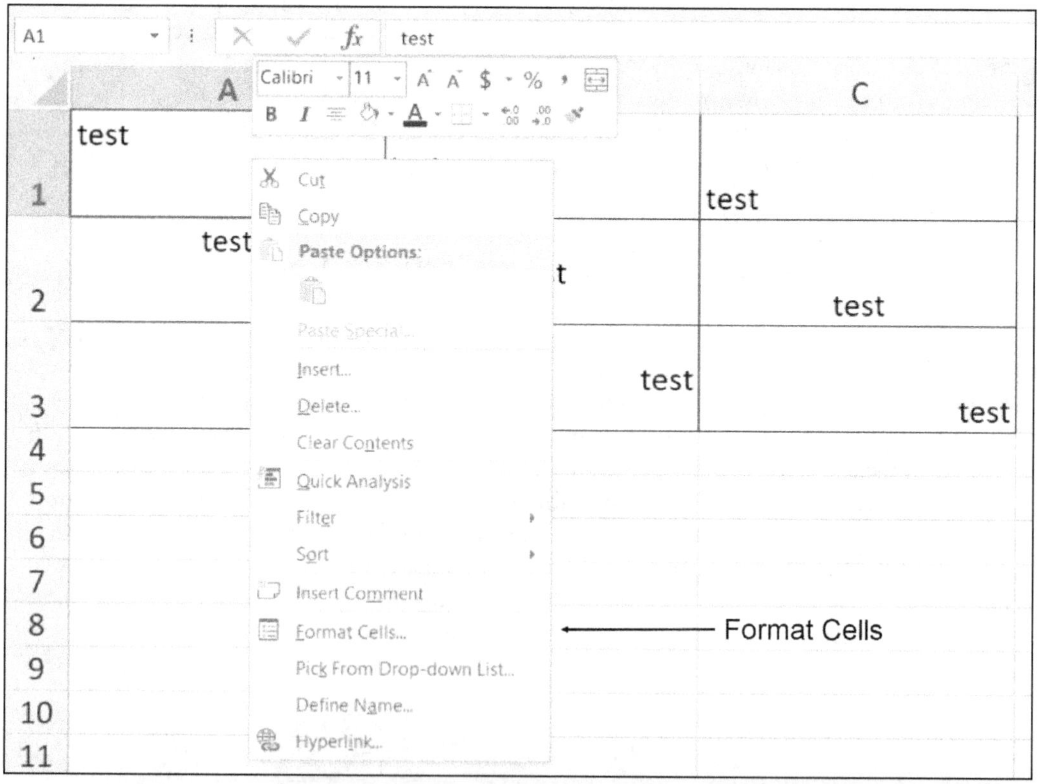

When the Format Cells dialogue box opens, go to the Alignment tab.

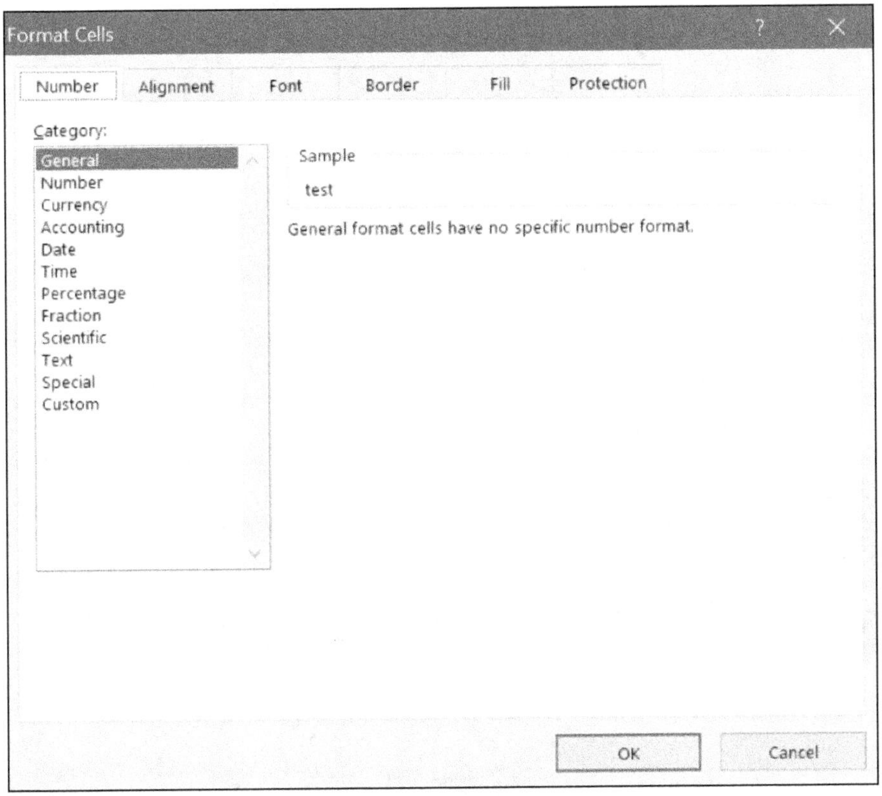

Choose from the Horizontal and Vertical dropdown menus to change the position of text within a cell (Top, Center, Bottom, Left, Right, etc.).

The Horizontal and Vertical dropdown menus have a few additional choices (like Justify and Distributed), but you generally shouldn't need them. (And be wary of Fill which it seems will repeat whatever you have in that cell over and over again until it fills the cell. Remember, if you do something you don't like, Ctrl + Z.)

You can also change the orientation of your text so that it's vertical or angled by entering the number of degrees (90 to make it vertical) or moving the line within the Orientation box to where you want it.

Bolding Text

You can bold text in a number of ways.

First, you can highlight the cell(s) you want bolded and click on the large capital B in the Font section of the Home tab.

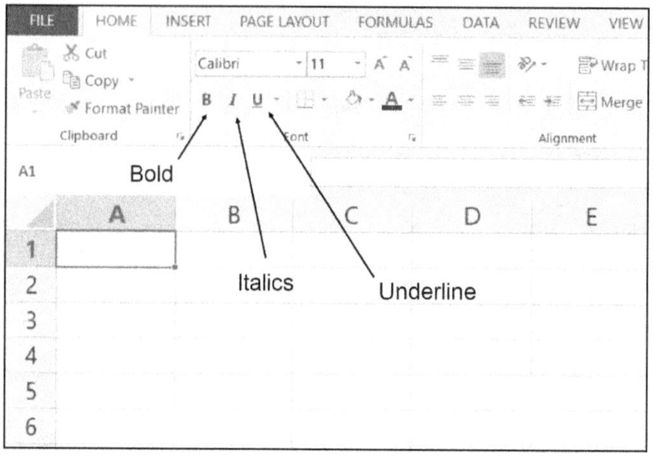

Second, you can highlight the cell(s) you want bolded and then type Ctrl and B at the same time. (Ctrl + B)

Or, third, you can highlight the cell(s) you want to bold and then right-click and choose Format Cells from the dropdown menu. Once you're in the Format Cells dialogue box, go to the Font tab and choose Bold from the Font Style options. If you want text that is both bolded and italicized, choose Bold Italic.

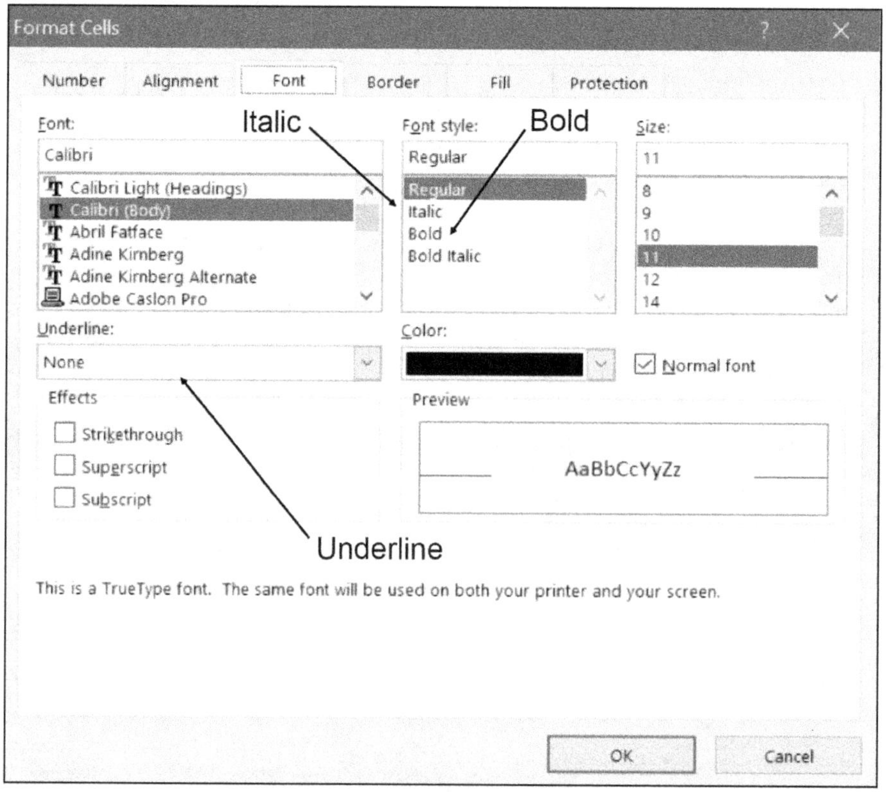

You can also bold just part of the text in a cell by clicking into the cell, highlighting the portion of the text that you want to bold, and then using any of the above methods.

To remove bolding from text or cells that already have it, highlight the bolded portion and then type Ctrl + B or click on the large capital B in the Font section of the Home tab. (If you happen to highlight text that is only partially bolded you may have to do it twice to remove the bold formatting.)

Borders Around Cells

It's nice to have borders around your data to keep the information in each cell distinct, especially if you're going to print your document.

There are two main ways to add borders around a cell or set of cells. First, you can highlight the cells you want to place a border around and then go to the Font section on the Home tab and choose from the Borders dropdown option. It's a four-square grid with an arrow next to it that's located between the U used for underlining and the color bucket used for filling a cell with color. Click on the arrow to see your available options, and then choose the type of border you want. (If you just want a simple border all around the cells and between multiple cells click on the All Borders option.)

With this option, to adjust the line thickness or line colors, see the options in the Draw Borders section, but be sure to choose your colors and line style before you choose your border type because the color and line type you choose will only apply to borders you draw after you choose them.

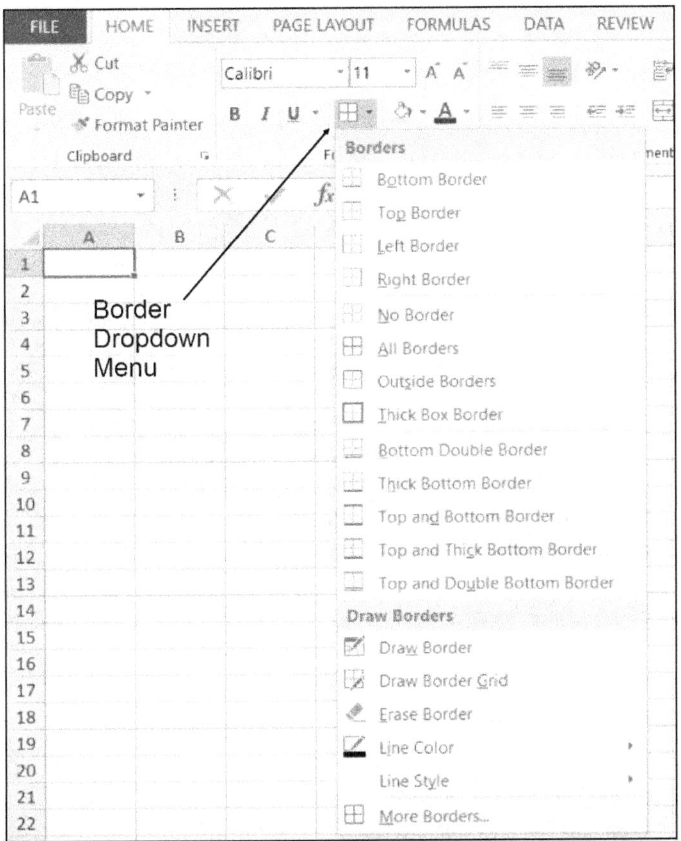

You can combine border types to get the appearance you want. For example, you could choose All Borders for the entire set of cells and then Thick Box Border to put a darker outline around the perimeter.

Your second choice is to highlight the cells where you want to place a border and then right-click and select Format Cells from the dropdown menu. Next, go to the Border tab and choose your border style, type, and color from there.

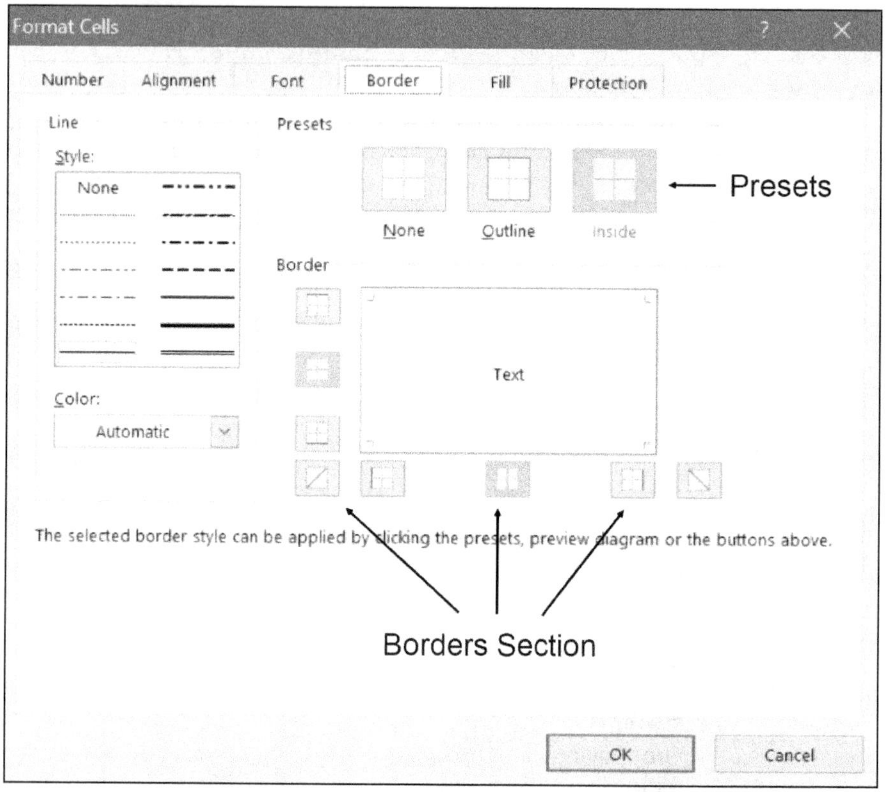

If you want one of the Preset options (outline or inside lines), just click on it. To clear what you've done and start over you can select None from the Presets section.

If you want only a subset of lines (for example, only the bottom of the cell to have a line), click on the choice you want from the Border section around the Text box. You can click on more than one of the lines in this section. So you could have, for example, a top and bottom border, but nothing else.

And, if you want to change the style of a line or its color from the default, you should do so in the Line section before you select where you want your lines to appear.

You can see what you've chosen and what it will look like in the sample box in the center of the screen.

Coloring a Cell (Fill Color)

You can color (or fill) an entire cell with almost any color you want. To do this, highlight the cell(s) you want to color, go to the Font section of the Home tab, and click on the arrow to the right of the paint bucket that has a yellow line under it. This should bring up a colors menu with 70 difference colors to choose from, including many that are arranged as complementary themes. If you want one of those colors, just click on it.

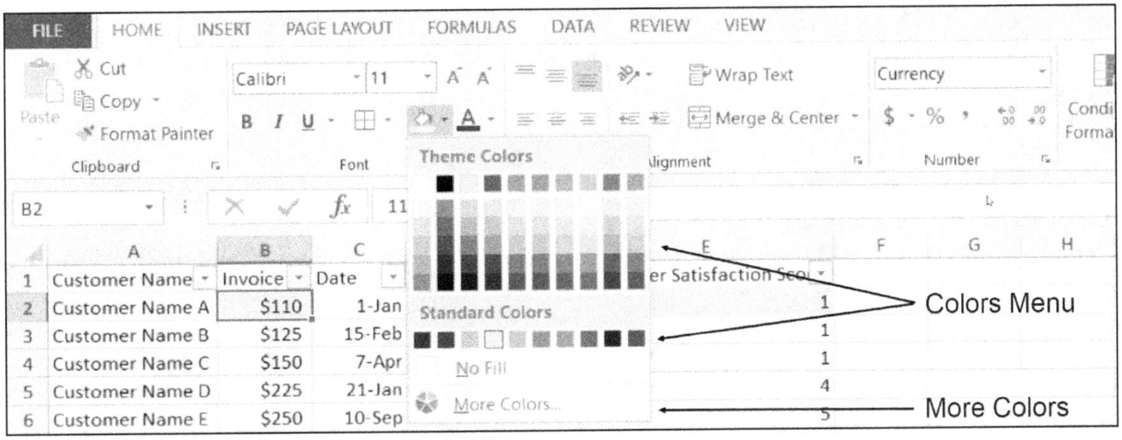

If none of those colors work for you, or you need to use a specific corporate color, click on More Colors at the bottom. This will bring up a Colors display box. The first tab of that box looks like a honeycomb and has a number of colors you can choose from by clicking into the honeycomb. The second tab is the Custom tab. It has a rainbow of colors that you can click on and also allows you to enter specific red, green, and blue values to get the exact color you need. (If you have a corporate color palette, they should give you the RGB values for each of the colors. At least my last employer did.)

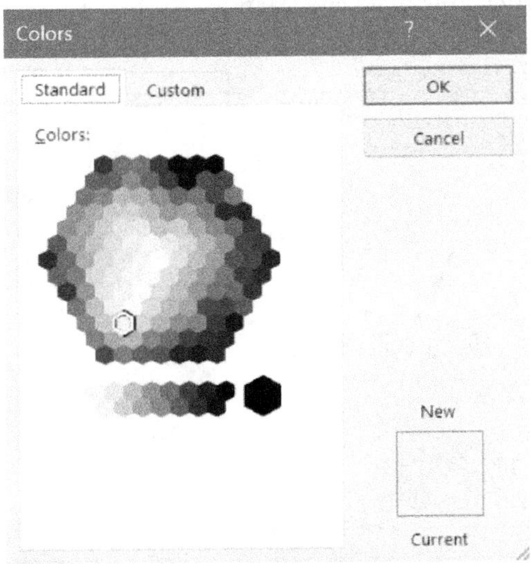

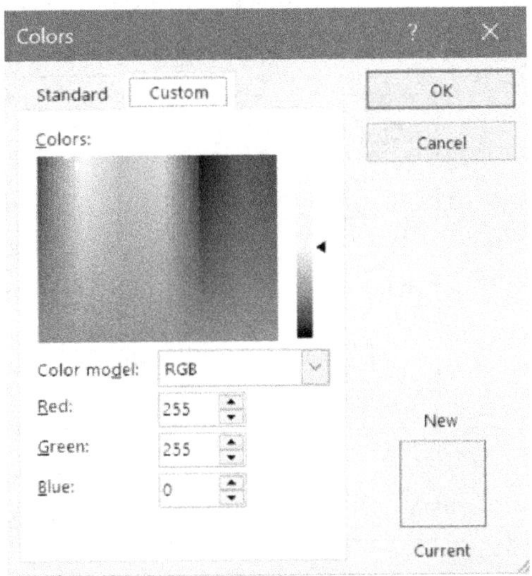

On the Custom tab, you can also use the arrow on the right-hand side to darken or lighten your color. With both tabs, you can see the color you've chosen in the bottom right corner. If you like your choice, click on OK. If you don't want to add color to a cell after all, choose Cancel.

Column Width (Adjusting)

If your columns aren't the width you want, you have three options for adjusting them.

First, you can right-click on the column and choose Column Width from the dropdown menu. When the box showing you the current column width appears, enter a new column width.

Second, you can place your cursor to the right side of the column name—it should look like a line with arrows on either side—and then left-click and hold while you move the cursor to the right or the left until the column is as wide as you want it to be.

Or, third, you can place your cursor on the right side of the column name and double left-click. This will make the column as wide or as narrow as the widest text currently in that column. (Usually. Sometimes this one has a mind of its own.)

To adjust all column widths in your document at once, you can highlight the entire worksheet and then double-left click on any column border and it will adjust each column to the contents in that column. (Usually. See comment above.)

To have uniform column widths throughout your worksheet, highlight the whole worksheet, right-click on a column, choose Column Width, and set your column width. Highlighting the whole worksheet and then left-clicking and dragging one column to the desired width will also work.

Currency Formatting

If you type a number into a cell in Excel, it'll just show that number. So, 25 is 25. $25 is $25. But sometimes you want those numbers to display as currency with the dollar sign and cents showing, too. Or you've already copied in unformatted numbers and now want them to have the same currency format.

To do this, highlight the cell(s) you want formatted this way, and then go to the Number section of the Home tab, and click on the $ sign.

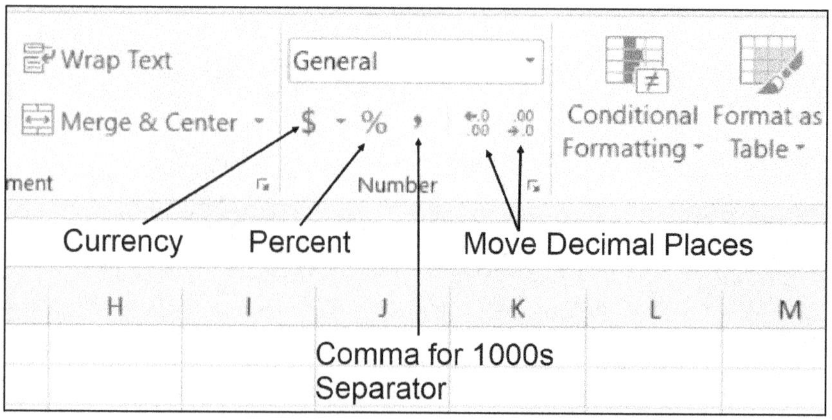

Another option is to highlight the cells you want formatted that way, go to the Number section of the Home tab, and use the dropdown to choose either Currency or Accounting.

You can also highlight the cell(s), right-click, choose the Format Cells option, go to the Number tab, and choose either Currency or Accounting from there.

Date Formatting

Sometimes Excel has a mind of its own about how to format dates. For example, if I type in 1/1 for January 1st, Excel will show it as 1-Jan. It means the same thing, but if I would rather it display as 1/1/2017, I need to change the formatting.

To do this, click on the cell with your date in it, go to the Number section on the Home tab, click on the dropdown menu, and choose Short Date. (You can also choose Long Date if you prefer that format.)

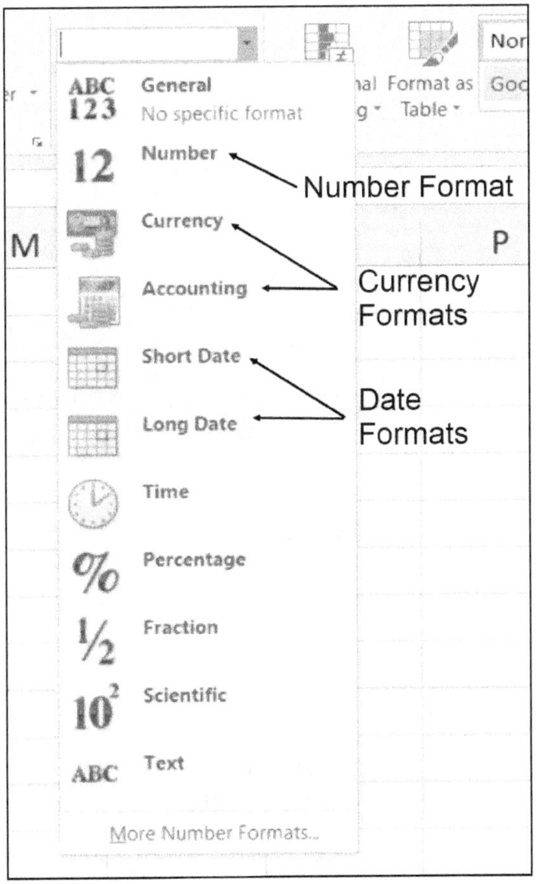

Another option is to highlight your cell(s), right click, choose Format Cells from the dropdown menu, go to the Number tab of the Format Cells dialogue box, and choose your date format from there by clicking on Date and then selecting one of the numerous choices it provides.

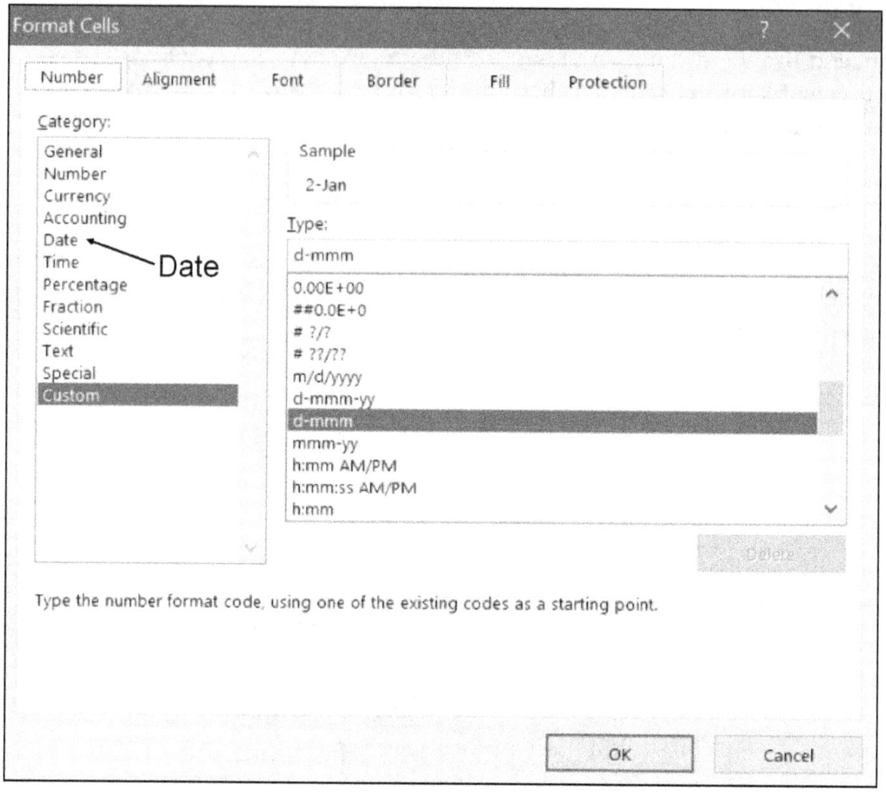

Note that if you just enter a month and day of the month like I did above, Excel will default to assuming that you meant the date to be for the current year and will store your date as MM-DD-YYYY even if you weren't trying to specify a year.

Font Choice and Size

In my version of Excel the default font choice is Calibri and the default font size is 11 point. You may have strong preferences about what font you use or work for a company that uses specific fonts for its brand or just want some variety in terms of font size or type within a specific document. In that case, you will need to change your font.

There are two ways to do this.

First, you can highlight the cells you want to change or the specific text you want to change, and go to the Font section on the Home tab. Select a different font or font size from the dropdown menus there.

You also have the option to increase or decrease the font one size at a time by clicking on the A's with little arrows in the top right corner that are next to the font dropdown box.

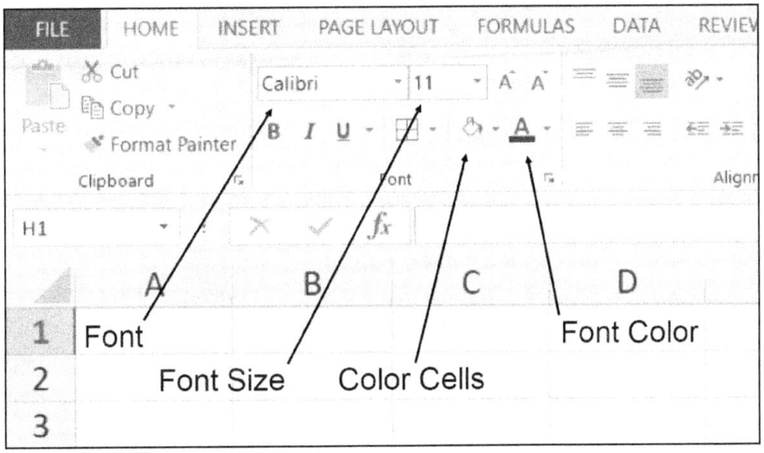

Second, you can highlight the cells or text you want to change, right-click, and choose Format Cells from the dropdown menu, and then go to the Font tab and choose your Font and Size from the listed values.

With either option, you can choose a font size that isn't listed by clicking into the font size box and typing the value you want.

Font Color

The default color for all text in Excel is black, but you can change that if you want or need to. (For example, if you've colored a cell with a darker color you may want to consider changing the font color to white to make the text in that cell more visible.)

You have two options. First, you can highlight the cells or the specific text you want to change, go to the Font section on the Home tab, and click on the arrow next to the A with a red line under it (see image above). You can then choose from one of the 70 colors that are listed, and if those aren't enough of a choice you can click on More Colors and select your color from the Colors dialogue box. (See Coloring a Cell for more detail about that option.)

Second, you can highlight the cell or text, right-click and choose Format Cells from the drop-down menu, go to the Font tab, and then click on the dropdown menu under Color which will bring up the same seventy color options and the ability to choose More Colors and add a custom color instead.

Italicizing Text

You do this by highlighting the cell(s) you want italicized and clicking on the slanted I in the Font section on the Home tab (see image under the Bolding description), or by highlighting the cell(s) and holding down the Ctrl key and the I key at the same time. (Ctrl + I)

Or, you can highlight the cell(s), right-click, choose Format Cells from the dropdown menu, go to the Font tab, and choose Italic from the Font Style options. (See image under the Bolding description.)

You can also italicize just part of the text in a cell by only selecting that portion and then using one of the methods above.

To remove italics from text or cells that already have it, you follow the exact same steps. (Highlight your selection and then type Ctrl + I or click on the slanted I in the Font section on the Home tab.)

Merge & Center

Merge and Center is a specialized command that can come in handy when you're working with a table where you want a header that spans multiple columns of data. (Don't use it if you plan to do a lot of data analysis with what you've input into the worksheet because it will mess with your ability to filter, sort, or use pivot tables. It's really for creating a finalized, pretty-looking report.)

If you're going to merge and center text, make sure that the text you want to keep is in the top-most and left-most of the cells you plan to merge and center. Data in the other cells that are being merged will be deleted. (You'll get a warning message to this effect if you have values in any of the other cells.)

You can merge cells across columns and down rows. So you could, for example, merge four cells that span two columns and two rows into one big cell while keeping all of the other cells in those columns and rows separate.

Highlight all of the cells you want to merge. Next, go to the Alignment section of the Home tab and choose Merge & Center. This will combine your selected cells into one cell and center the contents from the topmost, left-most cell that was merged across the selection.

You'll see on that dropdown that you can also choose to just Merge Across (which will just merge the cells in the first row) or to Merge Cells (which will merge the cells but won't center the text).

Also, if you ever need to unmerge those merged cells you can do so by selecting the Unmerge Cells option from that dropdown.

You can also Merge Cells by highlighting the cells, right-clicking, selecting the Format Cells option, going to the Alignment tab, and then choosing to Merge Cells from there. If you choose that option, you have to center the text separately.

Number Formatting

Sometimes when you copy data into Excel it doesn't format it the way you want. For example, I have a report I receive that includes ISBN numbers which are 10- or 13- digit numbers. When I copy those into Excel, it sometimes displays them in Scientific Number format (9.78E+12) as opposed to as a normal number.

To change the formatting of your data to a number format, you have two options.

First, you can highlight the cell(s) and go to the Number section of the Home tab. From the drop-down menu choose Number. (Sometimes General will work as well.) It will then convert it to a number with two decimal places. So 100.00 instead of 100. You can then use the zeroes with arrows next to them that are below the drop-down box to adjust how many decimal places display. The one with the right-pointing arrow will reduce the number of decimal places. The one with the left-pointing arrow will increase them. (See the Currency Formatting section for an image.)

Second, you can highlight the cell(s), right-click, select Format Cells from the dropdown, go to the Number tab, choose Number on the left-hand side listing, and then in the middle, choose your number of decimal places. You can also choose whether to use a comma to separate out your thousands and millions and how to display negative numbers at the same time.

Percent Formatting

To format numbers as a percentage, highlight the cell(s), and click on the percent sign in the Number section of the Home tab.

You can also highlight the cell(s), right-click, select Format Cells from the dropdown, go to the Number tab, choose Percentage on the left-hand side, and then in the middle, choose your number of decimal places.

Row Height (Adjusting)

If your rows aren't the correct height, you have three options for adjusting them. First, you can right-click on the row you want to adjust, choose Row Height from the dropdown menu, and when the box showing you the current row height appears, enter a new row height.

Second, you can place your cursor along the lower border of the row number until it looks like a line with arrows above and below. Left-click and hold while you move the cursor up or down until the row is as tall as you want it to be.

Third, you can place your cursor along the lower border of the row, and double left-click. This will fit the row height to the text in the cell. (Usually.)

To adjust all row heights in your document at once you can highlight the entire worksheet and then double-left click on any row border and it will adjust each row to the contents in each individual row. (Usually.) To have uniform row heights throughout your worksheet, you can highlight the whole sheet, right-click on a row, choose Row Height and set your row height that way or select the entire worksheet, right-click on the border below a row, and adjust that row to the height you want for all rows.

Underlining Text

You have three options for underlining text. First, you can highlight the cell(s) you want underlined and click on the underlined U in the Font section on the Home tab. (See the Bolding section for a screen shot.)

Second, you can highlight the cell(s) and type Ctrl and U at the same time. (Ctrl + U)

Third, you can highlight the cell(s), right-click, choose Format Cells from the dropdown menu, go to the Font tab, and choose the type of underlining you want (single, double, single accounting, double accounting) from the Underline drop down menu.

You can also underline part of the text in a cell by clicking into the cell, highlighting the portion of the text that you want to underline, and then using any of the above methods.

To remove underlining from text or cells that already have it, highlight the text and then use one of the above options.

Wrapping Text

Sometimes you want to read all of the text in a cell, but you don't want that column to be wide enough to display all of the text. This is where the Wrap Text option becomes useful, because it will keep your text within the width of the column and display it on multiple lines by "wrapping" the text.

(Excel does have a limit as to how many rows of text it will display in one cell, so if you have any cells with lots of text in them, check to make sure that the full contents of the cell are actually visible. You may have to manually adjust the row height to see all of the text.)

To Wrap Text in a cell, select the cell(s), go to the Alignment section of the Home Tab, and click on the Wrap Text option in the Alignment section.

Or you can highlight the cell(s), right-click, choose Format Cells from the dropdown menu, go to the Alignment tab there, and choose Wrap Text under Text Control.

* * *

One final formatting trick to share with you that is incredibly handy. (Maybe more so in Word than in Excel, but I use it frequently in both.)

Copying Formatting From One Cell To Another

In addition to the specific formatting options discussed above, if you already have a cell formatted the way you want it to, you can "Format Sweep" from that cell to other cells you want formatted the same way. You do this by using the Format Painter in the Clipboard section of the Home tab.

Highlight the cell(s) that have the formatting you want to copy (if the formatting is identical, just highlight one cell), click on the Format Painter, and then click into the cell(s) you want to copy the formatting to. The contents in the destination cell will remain the same, but the font, font color, font size, cell borders, italics/bolding/underlining, and text alignment and orientation will all change to match that of the cell that you swept the formatting from.

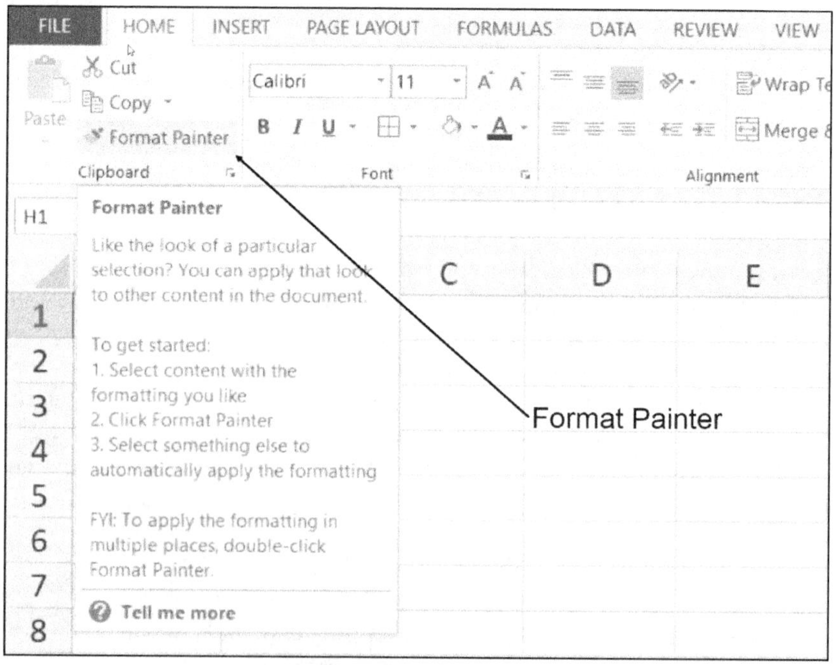

You need to be careful using the format sweeper because it will change *all* formatting in your destination cells. So, if the cell you're copying the formatting from is bolded and has red text, both of those attributes will copy over even if all you were trying to do was copy the bold formatting. (This is more of a problem when using the tool in Word than in Excel, but it's still something to watch out for especially if you have borders around cells.)

Also, the tool copies formatting to whatever cell you select next, which can be a problem if the cell you're copying from isn't next to the one you're copying to. Do not use arrow keys to navigate between the cells. You need to click directly from the cell with the formatting you want to the cell you're transferring the formatting to.

(Remember, Ctrl + Z is your friend if you make a mistake.)

If you have more than one isolated cell that you need to apply formatting to, you can double-click the Format Painter and it will continue to copy the formatting of the original cell to every other cell you click in until you click on the Format Painter again or hit Esc. (You'll know the tool is still in operation because there will be a little broom next to your cursor.)

You can copy formatting from multiple cells to multiple cells, so say the formatting for an entire row to an entire other row, but be sure to double-check the results since this is much more likely to result in unintended formatting.

Also, you can copy formatting from one cell to multiple cells at a time by simply highlighting all of the cells you want to copy the formatting to at once.

If you format sweep and then undo, you'll see that the cell(s) you were trying to format from are surrounded by a dotted border as if you had copied the cells. Be sure to hit the Esc key before you continue.

MANIPULATING YOUR DATA

Once you've entered your data into a worksheet, you might want to do something with it. Like sort it or filter it so you see only the entries that meet specific criteria, or analyze it using mathematical functions like addition or subtraction. This section will walk you through the basics of sorting, filtering, and analyzing your data.

Sorting

Sorting allows you to display your information in a specific order. For example, by date, value, or alphabetically. You can also sort across multiple columns, so you can, for example, sort first by date, then by name, then by amount.

To sort your data, select all cells that contain your information, including your header row if there is one.

If you set your data up with the first row as the header and all of the rest as data, you can just click in the top left corner of your worksheet to select all of the cells in the worksheet. Excel will then figure out the limits of your data when you choose to sort.

If you have a table of data that starts lower down on the page or that has a summary row or that is followed by other data, be sure to only select the cells in the data set you want to sort, because Excel will sort everything you select whether it makes sense to do so or not.

Once you've selected your data, go to the Editing section of the Home tab. Click on the arrow next to Sort & Filter, and choose Custom Sort. Your other option is to go to the Data tab and click on the Sort option there. Either path will bring you to the Sort dialogue box.

The first choice you need to make is to indicate whether or not your data has headers. In other words, does the first row of your data contain column labels? If so, click on that box in the top corner that says, "My data has headers." If you indicate that there is a header row, it will not be included in your sort and will remain the first row of your data.

When you do this, you'll see that your Sort By dropdown now displays your column labels. If you don't check this box, the dropdown will show generic column names (Column A, Column B, etc.) and all of your data will be sorted, including the first row.

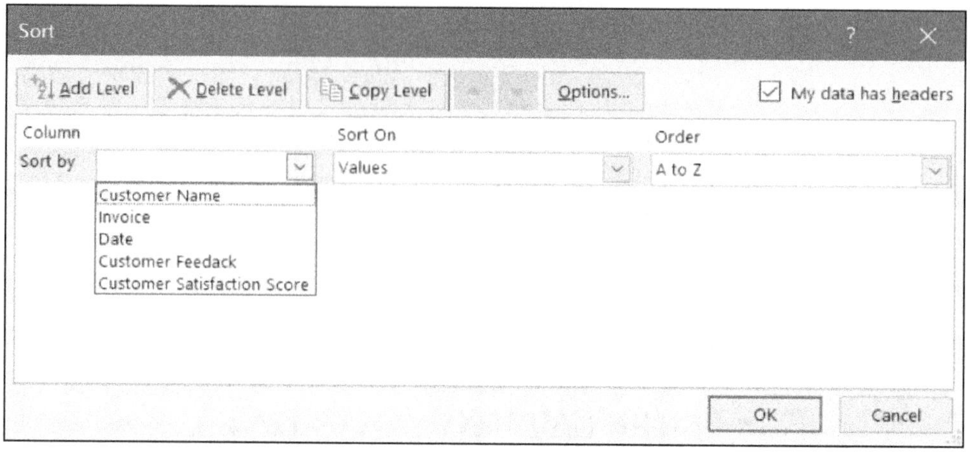

Sometimes Excel tries to decide this for you and is wrong, so always make sure that your Sort By choices make sense given the data you selected, and that you check or uncheck the "My data has headers" box to get the result you want.

The next step is to choose your sort order.

What is the first criteria you want to sort by? Chose that column from the Sort By dropdown menu.

Next, choose *how* to sort that column of data. You can sort on values, font color, cell color, and icon. I almost always use values.

After that, choose what order to use. For text it's usually from A to Z to sort alphabetical or from Z to A to sort reverse alphabetical. I also sometimes use the Custom List option when I have a column with the months of the year or the days of the week in it. For numbers it's just Smallest to Largest or Largest to Smallest.

If all you want to sort by is one column, then you're done. Click OK.

If you want to sort first by the column you already entered and then by another column, you need to add the second column. Click on Add Level and select your next column to sort by and your criteria for that sort.

If you add a level you don't need, highlight it and choose Delete Level.

If you have multiple levels but decide that they should be sorted in a different order, you can use the arrows to the left of Options to move a sort level up or down.

The default is to sort top to bottom, but you can click on Options to sort left to right or to make your sort case sensitive.

When you're done with your sort options, click OK. If you change your mind, click Cancel. If you get a sort that has a mistake in it, remember to use Ctrl + Z to undo and try again.

A few things to watch out for with sort order. Be sure that you've selected all of the data you want sorted. If you only highlight three columns but have six columns of data, only the first three columns will be sorted. The other three columns will stay in their original order which will break the relationship between your data points.

Excel also offers quick-sort options (the ones that say Sort A to Z or Sort Z to A), but be wary when using them. Sometimes they work great, most times they sort in the wrong order for me or on the wrong column or miss that I have a header row. To save myself time and effort, I usually just use Custom Sort instead.

Filtering

Sometimes you want your data to stay right where it is, but you want to see only certain results that meet a specific criteria. For example, only customers located in Mozambique. Filtering allows you to do that. As long as your data is displayed in rows (and ideally with contiguous columns), you can use filtering.

To start, click on any cell in the header row of your data, and then in the Editing section of the Home tab, click on the arrow next to Sort & Filter and choose Filter.

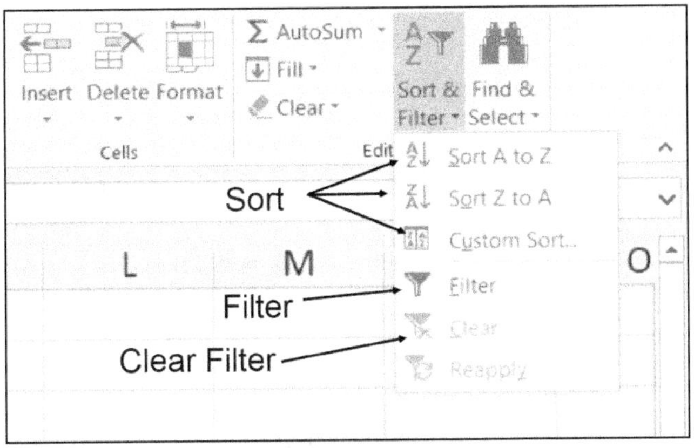

You should now see gray arrows to the right of each label in your first row.

One thing to note here is that the Filter function will only show arrows for columns that are touching. So if you have data in Columns A through D and then in Columns F through K, it will show the filter arrows for either Columns A through D OR Columns F through K, but not for both sets of columns at the same time. If you want to be able to filter on all of those columns at once, you need to remove any blank columns in between.

What I'm about to discuss applies to more recent versions of Excel, but not older versions. As I recall, older versions basically let you filter on one column and with limited criteria. You certainly couldn't filter by color until very recently. So if you have an older version of Excel you may be able to filter your results some, but not as well as with more recent versions. And if you save into an older version of Excel while your data is filtered, you may experience issues with how your data displays. If I recall correctly it keeps the filtering you had in place, but doesn't show all of the filtering choices you made. (I usually don't keep filters on my data. I use filtering to view my data while I'm working, but then I remove them before I close the file.)

Okay. Back to how to filter.

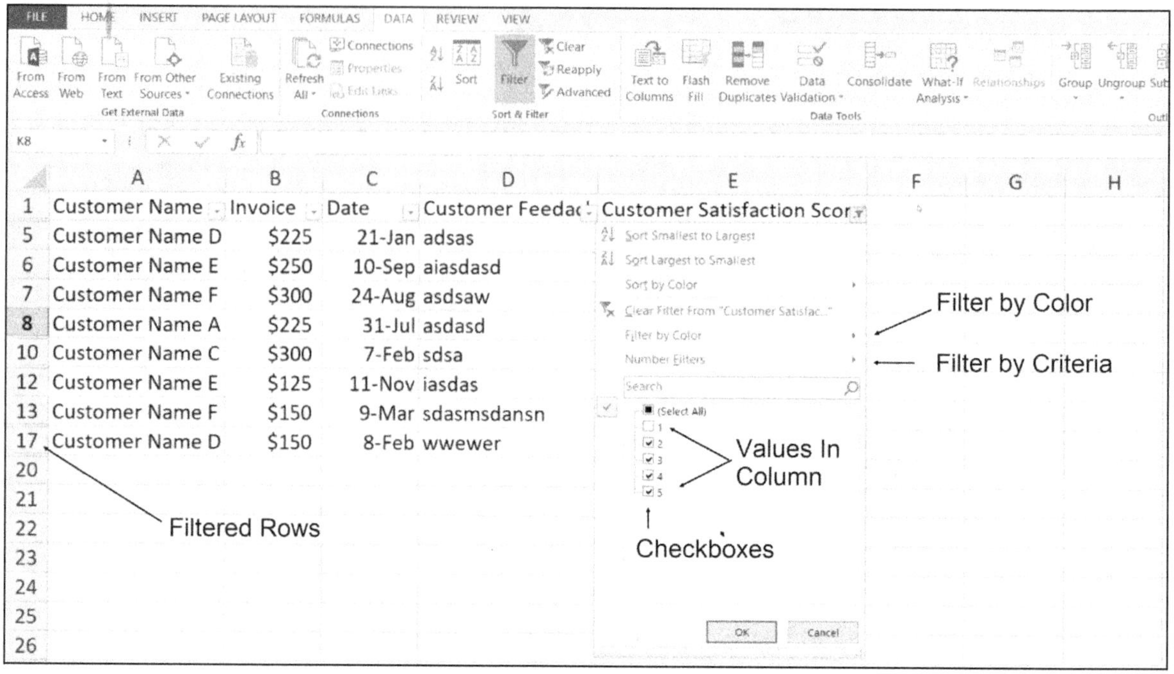

If you click on the arrow for any given column, you should see a list of all potential values in that column with checkboxes next to each value. For really long data sets (tens of thousands of rows) this may not be a complete listing. It definitely wasn't in older versions of Excel.

For basic filtering, you can use the checkboxes to set the criteria for what data to display. Simply uncheck the box for any values you don't want to see.

Or, if you want to see only one or two of the values, what you can do is click in the Select All box to unselect all of the values, and then click in the box for the one or two you want to see.

You can also type the name of the value you want to filter by into the Search field.

Or you can filter by criteria instead. Depending on the type of data you're filtering, the option will say Number Filters or Text Filters.

Click on the arrow and you should see options like "Equals" or "Does Not Equal" or "Begins With" or "Between" etc. The options differ depending on whether it's text or a number. You can use these filter criteria to select only the rows where those criteria are met. So, for example, you can filter to include only invoices over $500 or only customers in Canada.

Or, invoices over $500 for customers in Canada. Current versions of Excel allow you to filter on multiple columns at once.

If you've color-coded cells using Font color or Cell color, you can also filter by those criteria, using the Filter by Color option.

When cells in your worksheet are filtered, the row numbers in your worksheet will be colored blue, and you'll see that the row numbers skip since some rows won't be displayed. (In the screenshot above, rows 2, 3, 4, 9, 11, 14, 15, and 16 have been filtered out because they had customer satisfaction scores of 1.)

Columns where filtering is in place will show a funnel instead of an arrow on the gray dropdown next to the column name.

To remove filtering from a specific column, click on the gray arrow, and select Clear Filter from [Column Name].

To remove all filtering in a worksheet, go to the Editing section of the Home tab, click on Sort & Filter, and then choose Clear.

* * *

Alright, that was sorting and filtering. Let's talk functions now.

For any function, start with an equals sign (=) in the cell. That tells Excel that you're calculating something in this cell and to look for a function or mathematical symbol (like a * for multiplication).

Excel has hundreds of functions but the ones you'll probably use the most are the basic math functions, so we'll start there.

Basic Math Functions

Basic math functions in my definition are addition, subtraction, multiplication, and division. The below image shows simple formulas for each of the four basic math functions. The first column is when two values are involved, the second column is for when multiple values are involved. We'll walk through each one in a second, but note that for addition and multiplication there are named functions that you can use (SUM and PRODUCT, respectively) when multiple values are involved, but there are no named functions for subtraction or division.

While all of the examples I'm about to use focus on data in one worksheet, you can perform functions across worksheets. It's the same process, just click on the cell you want to use in the worksheet where it's located and Excel will take care of the rest.

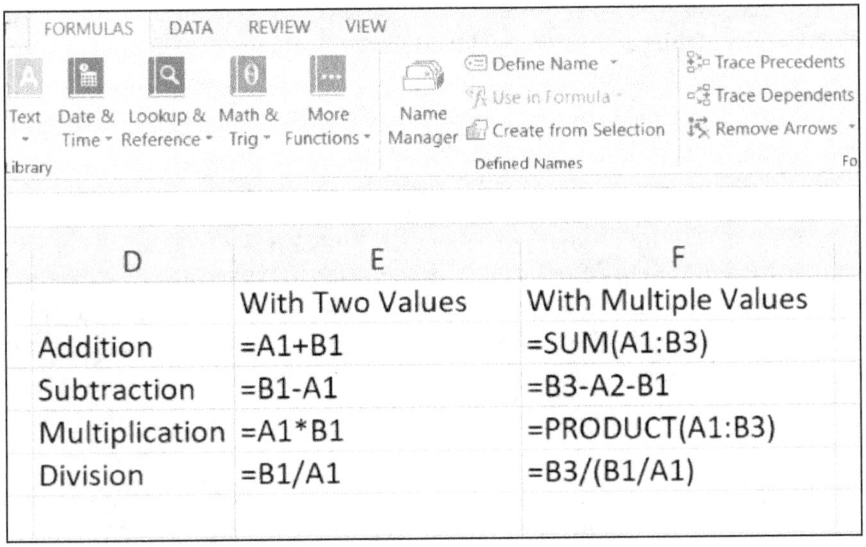

D	E	F
	With Two Values	With Multiple Values
Addition	=A1+B1	=SUM(A1:B3)
Subtraction	=B1-A1	=B3-A2-B1
Multiplication	=A1*B1	=PRODUCT(A1:B3)
Division	=B1/A1	=B3/(B1/A1)

Alright, let's walk through each one in more detail.

Addition

If you just want to know what the value of some cells added together is, but you don't need it recorded in your worksheet, you actually don't even need to use a function. You can just highlight the cells you want to add together and then look in the bottom right corner of the worksheet. It should show you the average, the count, and the sum of the cells you have highlighted.

But if you want the results of that addition visible in a cell in the worksheet, then you need to use either the + sign or the SUM( ) function.

The + sign tells Excel to add the two values on each side of the sign together. So above where it says =A1+B1 that's telling Excel to add the values in cell A1 and cell B1. You can also write it as =25+35 and have Excel add 25 to 35. You don't have to use cell references, but remember that normally in Excel all you'll see displayed is the result of a calculation. The only way to know what values were combined is to click on the specific cell and look in the formula bar.

If you have more than one value to add together, you can use the SUM function. The easiest way to do this is to type

=SUM(

into your cell and then highlight the cells you want to add together. Excel will convert the cells you've highlighted into the proper notation.

As you can see above, the formula for the example is =SUM(A1:B3). This is adding cells A1, B1, A2, B2, A3, and B3 together. Rather than try to figure out the proper way to summarize that, it's best to let Excel do it. But if you want to do it yourself, basically a colon between cells (:) means "through" and a comma (,) means "and." So =SUM(A1,B3) would mean add A1 to B3.

Also, to reference an entire column leave out the row references. So =SUM(B:B) means sum all of the values in column B. And =SUM(B:C) means sum all of the values in columns B and C.

If you want to make sure that you entered your formula correctly, note that when you type a formula into Excel it will highlight the cells included in the formula.

To check the contents of a formula later, double-click on the cell with the formula and Excel will highlight the cells being used, and will color-code them as well. (Very helpful with nested IF functions, which are covered in the *Intermediate Excel* guide.)

With addition, you also have one other option. You can use the AutoSum option in the Editing section of the Home Tab. This is basically just another way to create your formula for you.

The AutoSum icon looks like the mathematical sum function (a big pointy E-like shape). Click in the cell either below or to the right of the numbers you want to add together, click on AutoSum, and Excel will highlight all contiguous numbers either above the cell or to the left of it, and create a SUM formula for you using those cells. The AutoSum option stops at blank lines, so if you need to sum across a blank space, you'll need to edit the formula for it to work.

Subtraction

There are no nifty shortcuts when it comes to subtraction. You basically just have to type in a formula using the negative sign. The basic format is =( )–( )–( ) where the parens represent your different values. So if I want to subtract the value in cell B1 from the value in cell A1 I would type =A1-B1.

If I want to subtract B1, C1, and D1 from A1 I could either type =A1-B1-C1-D1 or I could also use the SUM function and type =A1-SUM(B1:D1) since that gets the same result.

As with any type of subtraction, be sure you get the numbers in the right order. The number you're starting with goes on the left-hand side, the number you're taking away from that goes on the right-hand side.

Also, you can still click on the cells you need instead of typing the whole formula. So, start with =, click on the first cell you need, type - , and click on the next one. Not as useful for subtraction as it is for addition, because you can't really use it with multiple cells at once.

Multiplication

Multiplication basically works the same way as addition. You can use the function PRODUCT or you can use the star symbol (*) between two values you want to multiply together.

So if you want to multiply cell A1 by cell B1, you'd type =A1*B1 or =PRODUCT (A1:B1) or =PRODUCT (A1, B1). All three formulas will get you the same result.

For multiple values, it would be =A1*B1*C1 or =PRODUCT (A1:C1) or =PRODUCT(A1,B1,C1).

Division

Division, much like subtraction, is another one where order matters. In the case of division you use the right slash (/) to indicate that the number on the left-hand side should be divided by the number on the right-hand side.

So if I want to divide A1 by B1, I would type =A1/B1.

It's best not to divide multiple numbers in one cell, because it's prone to error and it's better to see your steps as you go, but if you do so, make sure to use parens to ensure that the correct numbers get divided since =(A1/B1)/C1 is different than =A1/(B1/C1).

Complex Formulas

As I just hinted, you can definitely do much more complex formulas in Excel. You just have to make sure you write it properly so that Excel knows which functions to perform first.

Put something in parens and Excel will do that before anything else. Otherwise it will follow standard mathematical principles about which actions to perform in which order.

According to the Excel help documentation (under Operator Precedence), Excel will first combine cells (B1:B3 or B1, B2), then create any negative numbers (-B1), then create percents, then calculate any exponentials (B2^2), then do any multiplication and division, then do any addition and subtraction, then concatenate any values, and then do any comparisons last.

All of this, of course, at least in the U.S., is done from left to right in a formula.

So, basically, Excel calculates starting on the left side of the equation and moves to the right, doing each of those steps above in that order throughout the entire formula before circling back to the start and doing the next step. Which means that multiplication and division are done first and then addition or subtraction.

Of course, anything in parens is treated as a standalone equation first. So if you have =3*(4+2), Excel will add the 4 and the 2 before it does the multiplication.

Basically, if you're going to write complex formulas they're definitely doable but you should be very comfortable with math and how it works. Also, be sure to test your equation to make sure you did it right. I do this by breaking a formula into its component steps and then making sure that my combined equation generates the same result.

Other Functions

Excel has a ton of available functions that can do all sorts of interesting things and not just with numbers.

To see what I'm talking about, go to the Formulas tab. There are seven different subject areas listed there (Financial, Logical, Text, Date & Time, Lookup & Reference, Math & Trig, and Other). Click on each of those dropdowns and you'll see twenty-plus functions for each one.

But how do you know if there's a function that does what you want to do? For example, is there a function for trimming excess space from a string of values? (Yes. It's called TRIM.) Or for calculating the cumulative principal paid on a loan between two periods? (Yes.)

So how do you find the function you want without hovering over each function to see what it does?

The simple way is to go to the Formulas tab and click on Insert Function. This will bring up the Insert Function dialogue box which includes a search function. Type a few words for what you're looking for.

For example, if I want to calculate how many days until some event occurs and I want to have this formula work no matter what day it is when I open my worksheet, then I need some way to set a value equal to today's date whatever day today is. So I search for "today" and get a function called TODAY that it says "Returns the current date formatted as a date." Perfect.

Or what if I have two columns of text and I want to combine them. If I search for "combine text" my second option is CONCATENATE which is described as "Joins several text strings into one text string." That'll work.

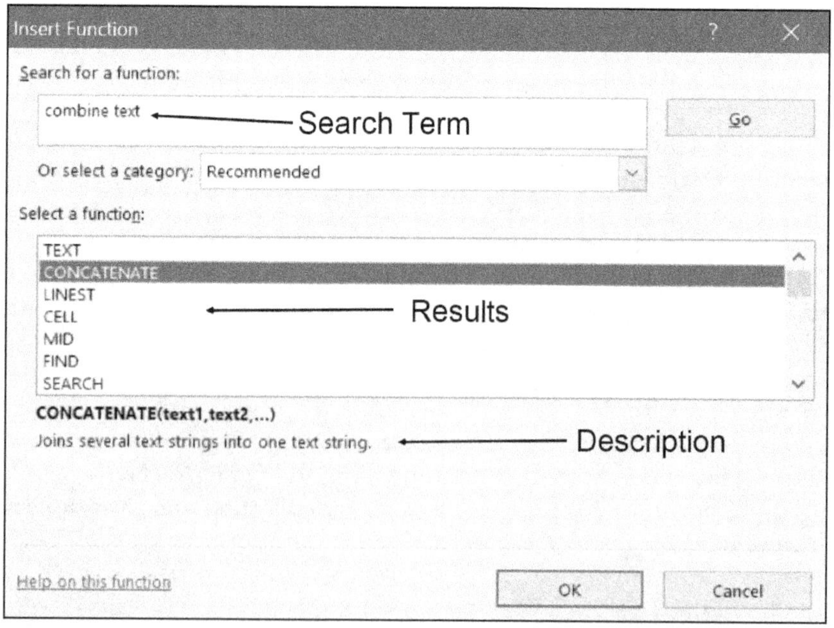

Once you've found a function you like, highlight it and click on OK. Excel will take you back to the worksheet and show you a Function Arguments dialogue box that tells you what inputs are needed to create that particular function.

So for CONCATENATE it shows me boxes for Text 1 and Text 2, because to write a concatenate function you need to at least write =CONCATENATE(A1, B1) where A1 and B1 are the two cells you're combining.

Sometimes selecting a function this way, even if you know what it does, is helpful because it shows you what order you need to put the information in and what form it needs to take. But you can also see this to a lesser degree when you start to type the function into your cell. Once you type the opening paren it will show you the components you need and their order. (Very helpful for things like SUMIF and SUMIFS that have different orders even though they do similar things.)

As a side note, TRIM, CONCATENATE, and SUMIFS are all discussed in further detail in *Intermediate Excel.*

Copying Cells With Formulas in Them

One of the nice things about working with formulas in Excel is that you don't have to type them over and over and over again. You can type a formula once and if you need to use it again, simply copy it to a new cell.

There are some tricks to copying formulas. So let's walk through those.

By default, formulas are relative. Meaning that if you have a formula that says =B1+C1 and you copy it (Ctrl + C) over to the right one cell it will become =C1+D1. If you copy it down one cell from that original location it will become =B2+C2. This is great when you have rows and rows of data with everything located in the same position and want to perform the exact same calculation on each of those rows. You can simply copy the formula and paste it down the entire column and it will perform that calculation on each and every row.

But sometimes you just want to move the calculation. Say it's in Cell B2 now and you want to put it in Cell A10. That's when you need to cut the formula (Ctrl + X) and move it instead of copy it. By cutting and moving the formula, it stays the exact same. If it said =B1+C1 it still does.

Another way to do this is to click into the cell, highlight all of the text in the cell, copy it, and tab (or Esc) out of the cell, and then click on the new location and paste it. (If you click into the cell, highlight all of the text, and try to click on where you want to paste it, you'll end up replacing your existing text in the source cell with a reference to the cell you clicked into.)

What if you want to copy the formula, but you want to keep some portion of it fixed. Either the row reference, the column reference, or the reference to an entire cell. (Useful when calculating different scenarios where you build a table with different values for variable x in one row and different values for variable y in one column and then calculate what value you get for each combination of x and y. So, hourly pay and hours worked, for example.)

You can fix a portion of a formula by using the $ sign. (We discussed it earlier with respect to inputting data, but I'll run through it again here.)

To fix the reference to a cell, put a $ sign before both the letter and the number in the cell name. So cell B2 becomes B2 in your formula. If you reference a cell that way (B2), no matter where you copy that formula to it will continue to reference that specific cell. This is useful if you have a constant listed somewhere that's used in a calculation performed for a number of rows. So say you're selling widgets and they're all priced at $100. You might list Widget Price at the top of your worksheet and put 100 in a cell at the top and then calculate how much each customer owes by multiplying their units purchased by that fixed value.

If you want to keep just the column the same, but change the row reference, put the dollar sign in front of the letter only. So $B2 when copied would become $B3, $B4, etc.

If you want to keep the row the same, but change the column reference, you'd put the dollar sign in front of the number only. So B$2. When copied, that portion of the formula would change to C$2, D$2, etc.

One more thought about copying formulas. I usually just highlight all of the cells where I want to copy the formula to and then paste, but there's a shortcut that you can sometimes use that's faster when you have many many rows of data.

If you have a formula in a cell and want to copy it downward and the column where that cell is located is touching another column of data that has already been completed (so you have a full column of data next to the column where you want to put your formula), you can place your cursor on the bottom right corner of the cell with the formula and double-left click. This should copy the formula down all of your rows of data.

It doesn't work if the other column of data hasn't been filled in yet. Excel only knows how far to copy the formula based on the information in the other column. But it can be a handy shortcut in a table with lots of completed information where you're just adding a calculation.

Select All

Another little trick that comes in handy when I'm working with data I've already added to my worksheet is the ability to select all of the contents of the worksheet at once. To do this, click on the top left corner of the sheet where the rows and columns meet. In this version of Excel the bottom half of the square is light gray.

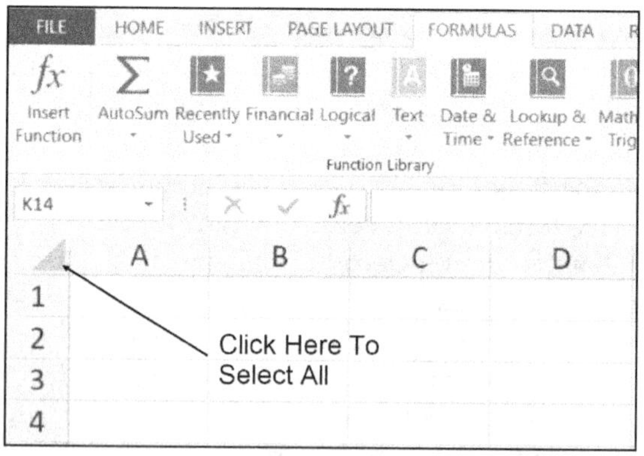

Doing this will select all of the rows and columns in the worksheet and allow you to easily copy the contents so you can move them to another worksheet. Usually I do this when I want to use the Paste Special – Values option to remove any formulas from the worksheet. I Select All, Copy, Paste Special-Values and that overwrites the entire worksheet with just that values that were in the cells.

PRINTING

Alright. That was the basics of manipulating your data. Now on to printing. You might not think that printing needs its own chapter, but it does. Not because clicking on Print is so hard to do, but because you need to format your data well to get it to print well. If you just hit print without thinking about how that information in your worksheet will appear on a page, you'll likely end up with pages worth of poorly-formatted garbage.

Now, it's possible you have no intent of printing anything, in which case, skip this chapter. But if you are going to print, let's try and waste as little paper as possible for you.

First things first. To print, go to the File tab and select Print. If you don't want to clean anything up, you can then just click on the big Print button right there on the page and be done with it.

Typing Ctrl and P at the same time (Ctrl + P) will also take you to the print screen which looks like this:

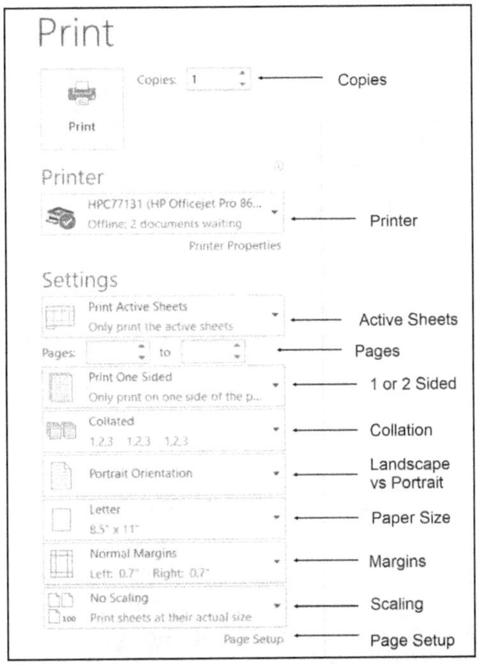

There are a number of things you can do on this page, so let's just walk through them starting at the top and working our way down.

Print

Once you're ready to print your page, you can click on the button on the top left with the image of a printer that says Print.

Number of Copies

If you want to print more than one copy, change your number of copies using the up and down arrows next to the Print button.

Printer

It should display your computer's default printer, but if you want to use a different printer than that one, click on the arrow next to the printer name and choose from the listed options. If the printer you want isn't listed, choose Add Printer and add the printer.

Print Active Sheets / Print Entire Workbook / Print Selection

My version of Excel defaults to Print Active Sheets. This will generally be the worksheet you were working in when you chose to print. However, you can select more than one worksheet by holding down the Control key and then clicking on another worksheet's name. When you do this, you'll see that the names of all of your selected worksheets are highlighted, not just one of them.

I would only print multiple worksheets if you're satisfied that each one is formatted the way you want it formatted. Also, choosing to print more than one sheet at a time either with Print Active Sheets or Print Entire Workbook, results in strange things happening to your headers and footers. For example, your page numbering will occur across worksheets. If you mean each worksheet to be a standalone report with numbered pages specific to that report, then you need to print each worksheet separately.

As I just alluded to, the Print Entire Workbook option prints all of the worksheets in your workbook.

Print Selection allows you to just print a highlighted section of a worksheet or worksheets. (I happened to have three worksheets selected at once and when I highlighted the first twenty cells in one of those worksheets, the selection it was ready to print was those twenty cells in each of the three worksheets.)

Print Selected Pages

Just below the Print Active Sheets section is a row that says Pages and has two boxes with arrows at the side. You can choose to just print a specific page rather than the entire worksheet. To figure out which page to print, look at your preview (which should be taking up most of the screen).

Print One Sided / Print on Both Sides (long edge) / Print on Both Sides (short edge)

The default is to just print on one side of your paper. If you have a printer that can print on both sides of the page you can change your settings to do so. You want the long-edge option if your layout is going to be portrait-style and the short-edge option if your layout is going to be landscape-style. (See below.)

Collated / Uncollated

This only matters if what you're printing has more than one page and if you're printing more than one copy. In that case, you need to decide if you want to print one full copy at a time, x number of times or if you want to print x copies of page 1 and then x copies of page 2 and then x copies of page 3 and so on until you've printed all pages of your document. In general, I would choose collated, which is also the default.

Portrait Orientation / Landscape Orientation

You can choose to print in either portrait orientation (with the short edge of the page on top) or landscape orientation (with the long edge of the page on top). You can see the difference by changing the option in Excel and looking at your print preview.

Which option you choose will depend mostly on how many columns of data you have.

Assuming I'm dealing with a normal worksheet with rows of data listed across various columns, my goal is to fit all of my columns on one page if possible. Sometimes changing the layout to landscape allows me to do that because it allows me to have more columns per page than I'd be able to fit in portrait mode.

If I have just a few columns of data, but lots of rows I'll generally stick with portrait orientation instead.

You'll have to decide what works best for you and your specific data.

Letter / Legal / Statement / Etc.

This is where you select your paper type. Unless you're in an office or overseas, chances are you'll leave this exactly like it is. I'm sure my printer could print on legal paper, but I don't have any for it to use so it's a moot point for me. In an office you may have the choice of 8.5"x11", legal paper, and even other larger sizes than that.

Normal Margins / Wide Margins / Narrow Margins / Custom Margins

I would expect you won't use this, but if you need to then this would be where you can change the margins on the document. The normal margins allow for .7" on each side and .75" on top and bottom. If you have a lot of text and need just a little more room to fit it all on one page, you could use the narrow margin option to make that happen. I generally use the scaling option instead.

No Scaling / Fit Sheet on One Page / Fit All Columns on One Page / Fit All Rows on One Page

I use this option often when I have a situation where my columns are just a little bit too much to fit on the page or my rows go just a little bit beyond the page. If you choose "Fit All Columns on One Page" that will make sure that all of your columns fit across the top of one page. You might still have multiple pages because of the number of rows, but at least everything will fit across one page.

Of course, depending on how many columns you have, this might not be a good choice. Excel will make it fit, but it will do so by decreasing your font size and if you have too many columns you're trying to fit on one page your font size may become so small you can't read it.

So be sure to look at your preview before you print. (And use Landscape Orientation first if you need to.)

Fit All Rows on One Page is good for if you have maybe one or two rows too many to naturally fit on the page.

Fit Sheet on One Page is a combination of fitting all columns and all rows onto one page. Again, Excel will do it if you ask it to, but with a large set of data you won't be able to read it.

Page Setup

The Page Setup link at the very bottom gives you access to even more options. As with everything else in the more modern versions of Excel, the most obvious options are the ones that are readily visible that we already discussed, but there are other options you have in formatting your page. If you click on the Page Setup link you'll be taken to the Page Setup dialogue box which is another way to choose all your print options. A few things to point out to you that I find useful:

1. **Scaling**
   On the Page tab you can see the scaling option once more. But the nice thing here is that you can fit your information to however many pages across by however many pages long. You're not limited to 1 page wide or 1 page tall. So say you have a document that's currently one page wide and four pages long but the last page is just one row. You can scale that document in the Page Setup dialogue box so that the document that prints is one page wide by three pages long and that last row is brought up onto the prior page.

2. **Center Horizontally or Vertically**
   On the Margins tabs there are two check boxes that let you center what you're printing either horizontally or vertically or both. I will often choose to center an item vertically. If I don't do that, it tends to looks off balance.

3. **Header/Footer**
   We're going to talk about another way to do this in a moment, but if you want to setup a header and/or a footer for your printed document you can do so here. The dropdown boxes that say (none) include a number of pre-formatted headers and footers for you to use. So if you just want the page number included, there should be a pre-formatted one that lets you do that. Same with including the worksheet name or file name in the header

or footer. As you look at each one it will show you examples of the actual text that will be included. You also have the option of customizing either the header or footer.

4. Sheet
The sheet tab has a couple of useful options, but I'm going to show you a different way to set these options because I find it easier to set them when I'm in the worksheet itself.

* * *

Page Layout Tab

If you exit out of the print option and go back to your worksheet, you'll see that one of the tabs you have available to use is called Page Layout. There are certain attributes that I set up here before I print my documents. Let's walk through them.

(Also, note that you can change margins, orientation, and size here just as easily as in the print preview screen.)

1. Print Area
If you only want to print a portion of a worksheet, you can set that portion as your print area by highlighting it, and then clicking on the arrow next to Print Area and choosing Set Print Area.

Only do it this way (as opposed to highlighting the section and choosing Print-Selection) if it's a permanent setting. Once you set your print area it will remain set until you clear it. You can add more data to your worksheet but it will never print until you change your print area or clear the setting.

I use this when I have a worksheet that has either a lot of extra information I don't want to print or where the formatting extends beyond my data and Excel keeps trying to print all those empty but formatted cells.

2. Breaks
You can set where a page break occurs in your worksheet. So say you have a worksheet that takes up four pages and you want to make sure that rows 1 through 10 are on a page together and then rows 11 through 20 are on a page together even though that's not how things would naturally fall. You can set a page break to force that to happen.

Personally, I find page breaks a challenge to work with, so I usually try to get what I need some other way.

3. Print Titles
This one is incredibly valuable. When you click on it, you'll see that it brings up the Page Setup box and takes you to the Sheet tab.

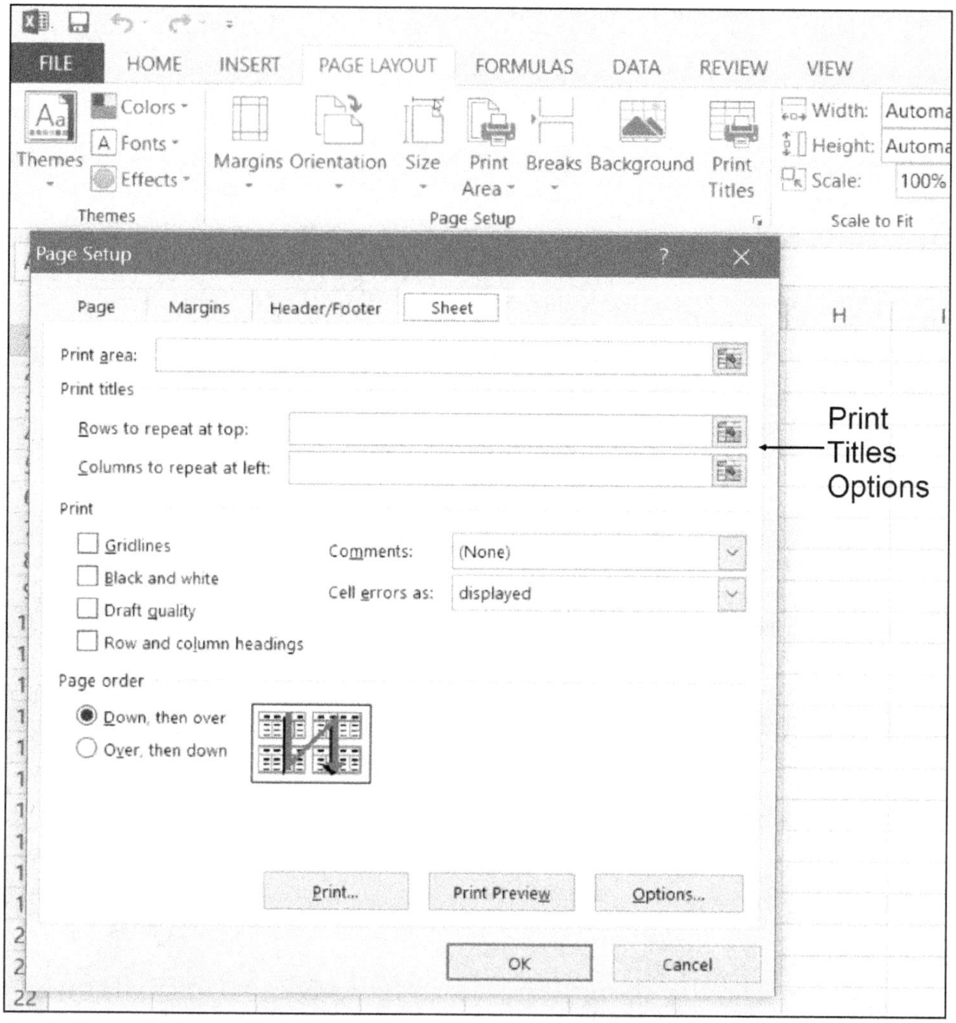

The first valuable thing you can do here is set the rows you want to repeat at the top of the page. Say you have a worksheet with a thousand rows of data in it that will print on a hundred pages. How do you know what's in each column on each page? You need a header row. And you need that header row to repeat at the top of each and every page.

"Rows to repeat at top" is where you specify what row(s) is your header row. Click in that box and then click on the row number in your worksheet that you want to have repeat at the top of each page.

The second valuable thing you can do here is set a column(s) you want to repeat on the left-hand side of each page. I need this one less often, but I do still sometimes use it. Say, for example, that you had a list of students, one per row, and their test scores across fifty tests, and that when you printed that information it printed across two pages. Well, without listing the student's name in the left-hand column on every page, you wouldn't know whose scores you were looking at after the first page. So you'd need to set that name column to repeat on each page.

To do so, click in the box that says "Columns to repeat at left", and then click on the letter for the column(s) you want to repeat on each page.

You'll see that Excel converts your choices to standard notation, so if you feel comfortable enough you can just type it in yourself, but I almost never do.

Do be careful if you're going to choose more than one row or column to repeat that you don't end up selecting so many rows or columns that you basically just print the same thing over and over and over again.

CONCLUSION

There you have it. A beginner's guide to Excel. This wasn't meant to be a comprehensive guide to Excel, but to instead give you the basics you need to do 95% of what you'll ever want to do in Excel. I hope it did that.

If something wasn't clear or you have any questions, please feel free to reach out to me at mlhumphreywriter@gmail.com. I don't check that email daily, but I do check it regularly and am happy to help.

Also, if there was something I didn't cover that you want to know about, the Microsoft website has a number of tutorials and examples that I think are very well-written and easy to follow at www.suppport.office.com. I usually find what I need with a quick internet search for something like "bold text Excel 2013" and then choose the Microsoft link

I find their web-based help much more useful than the Help options available within Excel, but you can try those, too. Click on the question mark in the top right corner and search for what you need. Or you can hold your mouse over the tasks listed on the various tabs and you'll usually see a brief description of what the item does. A lot of the descriptions also have a "tell me more" link at the bottom of the description that will take you directly to the help screen related to that item.

If you want to explore more advanced uses of Excel and liked the way I present information, then check out *Intermediate Excel* which explores topics such as pivot tables, charts, conditional formatting, IF functions, and a lot more. (The full list is included in the introduction to the book.)

I've also published a few hands-on guides that might interest you.

The *Juggling Your Finances: Basic Excel Primer* focuses on how to use addition, subtraction, division, and multiplication to manage your personal finances and walks you through a number of sample calculations. The focus there is just on those four functions and how to use them.

Excel for Writers and *Excel for Self-Publishers* are geared towards writers and assume that you're comfortable with Excel. They walk users through exactly how to create things like a word count and time tracker or a two-variable analysis grid right down to how to format the cells to match the examples and what each formula needs to be in each cell. Sometimes the challenge with Excel is in figuring out how to use it to do what you want and that's what those guides cover.

Again, if there's something specific you want to know how to do, just ask. Happy to point you in the right direction.

And thanks for reading this guide. Excel is an incredibly powerful tool and now that you have the foundation you need to use it effectively, I hope you'll see just how incredible it can be.

Also, if you want to test your knowledge of this material check out *The Excel for Beginners Quiz Book* which contains quizzes for each section of this book as well as five exercises that will allow you to apply what you've learned here in real-world scenarios.

INDEX

INDEX (CONTINUED)

CONTROL SHORTCUTS

For each of the control shortcuts, hold down Ctrl and the key listed to perform the command.

Command	Ctrl +
Select All	A
Bold	B
Copy	C
Find	F
Replace	H
Italicize	I
Print	P
Next Worksheet	Page Down
Prior Worksheet	Page Up
Save	S
Underline	U
Paste	V
Cut	X
Redo	Y
Undo	Z

ABOUT THE AUTHOR

M.L. Humphrey is a former stockbroker with a degree in Economics from Stanford and an MBA from Wharton who has spent close to twenty years as a regulator and consultant in the financial services industry.

You can reach M.L. at mlhumphreywriter@gmail.com or at mlhumphrey.com.

Owning Your Vision

by Clement Portlander

Original title:
Owning Your Vision

Editor: Kristo Villem
ISBN 978-9916-720-70-7

In the land of Aestoria, nestled among the rolling hills and green meadows, there lived a young girl named Leona. She had long, curly hair that cascaded down her back and big, bright eyes that sparkled like the stars. Leona was a dreamer and she spent most of her days lost in her imagination, imagining all the things she could be, all the adventures she could go on.

One day, Leona came across an old, wise woman who was sitting under a tree. The woman noticed Leona's dreamy expression and asked her what she was thinking about. Leona told her all about the amazing things she wanted to do, the places she wanted to see, and the people she wanted to meet. The wise woman listened carefully and then said, "Leona, all those things are possible, but you have to believe in yourself and your dreams first."

With those words in mind, Leona set out to follow her dreams. She wanted to be a painter, and she spent hours each day practicing her craft. She painted pictures of the world as she saw it, with bright colors and bold lines. But soon, Leona realized that her paintings were missing something. They lacked the magic and wonder that she saw in her imagination. So she set out to find a way to capture the true essence of her visions.

Leona travelled to the farthest corners of the world, seeking out the most talented artists and craftsmen. She studied with them, learning their techniques and honing her skills. But still, her paintings lacked the magic that she wanted. She began to feel discouraged, and wondered if she would ever be able to truly capture her vision.

One day, Leona met a wise old man who lived high up in the mountains. The man had a twinkle in his eye and a knowing smile on his lips. He told Leona that the secret to capturing her vision was not in the techniques she had learned, but in the way she saw the world. He told her that the magic she was looking for was already within her, and all she had to do was trust herself.

With renewed confidence, Leona set out to paint once again. She put all the techniques and knowledge she had learned aside, and let herself be guided by her heart. She painted the world as she saw it, with all its beauty and magic. And when she was done, she realized that the old man was right – the magic was already within her.

Leona became a famous painter, known throughout the land for her unique and beautiful paintings. People from all over would come to see her work, and she was even invited to paint a mural in the royal palace. And while she was proud of her achievements, she knew that the real victory was in owning her vision, and believing in herself.

Years passed, and Leona grew old. She had many apprentices who learned from her, and they too became famous painters. But Leona knew that her greatest achievement was not in her paintings, but in the way she had lived her life. She had owned her vision, and in doing so, had inspired countless others to do the same.

As Leona lay on her deathbed, she closed her eyes and whispered to herself, "I have lived a good life. I have owned my vision, and now it is time for me to rest. But the world will always be filled with dreamers, and I know that they will carry on the legacy of owning their own vision, just as I have done."

And with those words, Leona passed on, leaving behind a legacy that would inspire generations to come.

Leona had overcome many obstacles to bring her vision to fruition. Her hard work and perseverance had paid off, and her kingdom was thriving under her leadership. However, she knew that her time was limited and that one day, she would have to pass on the torch to someone else.

As the years went by, Leona searched high and low for someone who shared her passion and drive. She interviewed countless candidates and even considered grooming her own children to take over. But she couldn't find anyone who truly embodied the qualities she believed were essential to lead her kingdom.

Just as Leona was beginning to lose hope, she received a message from a neighboring kingdom. The message was from a young woman named Lyra who had heard about Leona's achievements and was interested in learning from her.

Leona was intrigued and invited Lyra to visit her kingdom. From the moment they met, Leona knew that Lyra was special. She was intelligent, compassionate, and had a strong sense of purpose. Over the course of several weeks, Leona and Lyra spent countless hours discussing their visions for the future and the challenges they faced.

Lyra was a quick study and absorbed everything that Leona taught her. She shadowed Leona as she went about her duties, and Leona was impressed by her ability to handle even the most difficult situations with grace and poise.

Eventually, Leona realized that Lyra was the one who could continue her legacy. She began to groom her as her successor, teaching her everything she knew and entrusting her with important responsibilities. Lyra proved to be an excellent leader, and under her guidance, the kingdom continued to prosper.

But as time passed, Leona grew weaker. She knew that her time was running out, and she feared for the future of her kingdom. However, she found comfort in knowing that she had passed on her vision to someone who could carry it forward.

On her deathbed, Leona called Lyra to her side. She spoke to her with pride and love, telling her how proud she was of her and how much she believed in her. With her final breath, Leona passed on her legacy to Lyra, knowing that she would lead the kingdom with the same strength and vision that had defined her own reign.

And so, Lyra took up the mantle of leadership, and under her guidance, the kingdom continued to thrive. She faced new challenges and obstacles, but with the wisdom and knowledge that Leona had passed on to her, she was able to overcome them all.

Years passed, and Lyra became known as one of the greatest rulers the kingdom had ever seen. Her name became synonymous with Leona's, and the legacy of these two powerful women lived on for generations to come. And as Lyra looked back on her life, she knew that it was her duty to pass on their vision to the next generation, so that their kingdom would continue to prosper for centuries to come.

The moral of the story "Owning Your Vision" is that it is important to have a clear vision and a sense of purpose in life. In order to achieve great things, one must have the courage to pursue their dreams, even in the face of adversity and obstacles.

The story also teaches the importance of mentorship and passing down knowledge and skills to the next generation. Through Leona's legacy, the next protagonist was able to learn from her and continue her work, ultimately making an even greater impact on the world.

Ultimately, the story highlights the importance of being true to oneself and staying true to one's values. The characters in the story were driven by a sense of purpose and a desire to make a positive impact on the world, and they were able to achieve their goals by staying true to their vision and their values. Ultimately, it is by owning our vision and being true to ourselves that we can make the greatest impact on the world.

CPSIA information can be obtained
at www.ICGtesting.com
Printed in the USA
LVHW061335140323
741532LV00019B/1126

9 789916 720707